Chicago Public Library

W9-ASR-967

Native Americans of the Southwest.

Native Americans of the Southwest

Stuart A. Kallen

Lucent Books, Inc.
P.O. Box 289011, San Diego, California

Titles in the Indigenous Peoples of North America Series Include:

The Apache
The Cherokee
The Iroquois
Native Americans of the Great Lakes
Native Americans of the Northeast
Native Americans of the Plains
Native Americans of the Southeast
Native Americans of the Southwest
The Navajo
The Sioux

Library of Congress Cataloging-in-Publication Data

Kallen, Stuart A., 1955–
    Native Americans of the Southwest / Stuart A. Kallen.
        p.   cm. — (Indigenous peoples of North America)
    Includes bibliographical references and index.
    Summary: Discusses the background, cultural practices, interaction
with Spanish settlers, and current lives of some of the native peoples
living in the American Southwest.
    ISBN 1-56006-681-4 (lib. bdg.)
    1. Indians of North America—Southwest, New—Juvenile literature.
[1. Indians of North America—Southwest, New.]   I. Title. II. Series.

E78.S7 K34 2000
979'.00497—dc21   99-050218

Copyright 2000 by Lucent Books, Inc.
P.O. Box 289011, San Diego, California 92198-9011

Printed in the U.S.A.

Contents

Foreword

North America's native peoples are often relegated to history—viewed primarily as remnants of another era—or cast in the stereotypical images long found in popular entertainment and even literature. Efforts to characterize Native Americans typically result in idealized portrayals of spiritualists communing with nature or bigoted descriptions of savages incapable of living in civilized society. Lost in these unfortunate images is the rich variety of customs, beliefs, and values that comprised—and still comprise—many of North America's native populations.

The *Indigenous Peoples of North America* series strives to present a complex, realistic picture of the many and varied Native American cultures. Each book in the series offers historical perspectives as well as a view of contemporary life of individual tribes and tribes that share a common region. The series examines traditional family life, spirituality, interaction with other native and non-native peoples, warfare, and the ways the environment shaped the lives and cultures of North America's indigenous populations. Each book ends with a discussion of life today for the Native Americans of a given region or tribe.

In any discussion of the Native American experience, there are bound to be similarities. All tribes share a past filled with unceasing white expansion and resistance that led to more than four hundred years of conflict. One U.S. administration after another pursued this goal and fought Indians who attempted to defend their homelands and ways of life. Although no war was ever formally declared, the U.S. policy of conquest precluded any chance of white and Native American peoples living together peacefully. Between 1780 and 1890, Americans killed hundreds of thousands of Indians and wiped out whole tribes.

The Indians lost the fight for their land and ways of life, though not for lack of bravery, skill, or a sense of purpose. They simply could not contend with the overwhelming numbers of whites arriving from Europe or the superior weapons they brought with them. Lack of unity also contributed to the defeat of the Native Americans. For most, tribal identity was more important than racial identity. This loyalty left the Indians at a distinct disadvantage. Whites had a strong racial identity and they fought alongside each other even when there was disagreement because they shared a racial destiny.

Although all Native Americans share this tragic history they have many distinct differences. For example, some tribes and individuals sought to cooperate almost immediately with the U.S. government while others steadfastly resisted the white presence. Life before the arrival of white settlers also varied. The nomads of the Plains developed altogether different lifestyles and customs from the fishermen of the Northwest coast.

Contemporary life is no different in this regard. Many Native Americans—forced onto reservations by the American government—struggle with poverty, poor health, and inferior schooling. But others have regained a sense of pride in themselves and their heritage, enabling them to search out new routes to self-sufficiency and prosperity.

The *Indigenous Peoples of North America* series attempts to capture the differences as well as similarities that make up the experiences of North America's native populations—both past and present. Fully documented primary and secondary source quotations enliven the text. Sidebars highlight events, personalities, and traditions. Bibliographies provide readers with ideas for further research. In all, each book in this dynamic series provides students with a wealth of information as well as launching points for further research.

Under the Turquoise Sky

The southwest region of the United States is a land of towering mesas, sheer cliff canyons, granite bluff mountains, and enormous scorching deserts under a stunning turquoise sky. But it is not a land that is hospitable to humans or animals. Temperatures reach 120 degrees in the summer and dip below freezing in the winter. Little rain falls in the region, but the natural balance of the ecosystem has been finely tuned over millions of years.

What people mean when they refer to "the Southwest" has changed over the years. Since the land became part of the United States in 1848, the term "Southwest" has come to encompass the present-day states of Arizona, New Mexico, the extreme southwestern corner of Colorado, the southern tip of Nevada, and southernmost Utah. California is not included in this region. The heart of the territory today is Arizona and New Mexico.

Because of the rugged terrain in this region, much of the area has been left in its natural state, even in the modern era. The Southwest is, however, the fastest-growing region in the United States, and the two major cities in the area—Phoenix, Arizona, and Las Vegas, Nevada—experienced record-setting population booms in the 1990s.

People of the Sun

When the Spanish arrived in the Southwest in the sixteenth century, the spectacular terrain was home to a diverse array of Native American tribes such as the Navajo, Pueblo, Apache, Maricopa, and the Tohono O'odham (also known as the Papago). Each tribe had its own distinctive culture and all had adapted to survival in the arid climate and rocky landscape over the course of several millennia. While Puebloan peoples such as the Hopi and Zuni lived settled lives in agricultural villages, southern tribes such as the Pima and Maricopa carved out an existence in one of the hottest, driest deserts in the world.

To these tribes, the awe-inspiring lands of the Southwest were nature's holy gift to the Native American people. The mountains, mesas, buttes, and canyons were believed to be the homes of gods, goddesses, and other supernatural spirits. These landmarks were to be protected, revered, worshipped, and used most respectfully. They were sacred places of physical healing and often provided life-giving food and water in an inhospitable desert environment.

A rich variety of Native American cultures developed in the Southwest, and the people who lived there were farmers, healers, warriors, astronomers, artists, storytellers, dancers, and more. Days were spent hunting and tending to corn crops in the fields; nights were enlivened by religious rituals and ceremonial performances. Most important, the people in the region lived in harmony with their natural surroundings, as described in 1929 by archeologist Edgar Lee Hewett:

Native Americans believed that the awe-inspiring lands of the Southwest were homes to gods, goddesses, and other supernatural spirits.

In his own Southwest the Indian is a harmonious element in a landscape that is incomparable in its nobility of color and mass and feeling of the Unchangeable. He never dominates it. . . . [H]e belongs there as do the mesas, skies, sunshine, spaces, and other living creatures. He takes his part in it with the clouds, winds, rocks, plants, birds and beasts, with drum beat and chant and symbolic gesture, keeping time with the seasons, moving in orderly procession with nature, holding to the unity of life in all things, seeking no superior place for himself but merely a state of harmony with all created things—the most rhythmic life as far as I know, that is lived among the races of men.[1]

Sunlight shines through the arch of Window Rock in Arizona. Native Americans believe that they live in harmony with their natural surroundings.

In order to exploit the region's natural resources, Conquistadors (pictured above) often used Native Americans as slave laborers.

Arrival of the Conquistadors

To the first Europeans in the region—Spanish conquerors, or conquistadors, who came north from Mexico in 1539—this unspoiled wilderness was something to be exploited, annexed, and tamed. They were looking for fabled cities glittering with gold and gems that they had heard about in rumor and legend. The Spaniards found no such cities, but they did find a place to plant their own crops, graze their cattle, and spread their religion to the natives, whose rich and diverse system of cultural beliefs they attempted to destroy.

The Spanish had four things never seen before by Native Americans that allowed the conquistadors to dominate the natives in the region: the horse, the wheel, the written word, and the gun.

For a short time the two cultures coexisted peacefully, but the heavy-handed tactics of the invaders soon touched off explosive conflicts. By the seventeenth century, European colonists were pouring into the region, settling on Native American lands, and demanding that the tribe members pay tribute to them in food, labor, and goods.

The Spaniards brought with them a host of diseases such as smallpox, measles, scarlet fever, and more to which the natives had little resistance. Epidemics swept across the lands, and some tribal populations were reduced by 75 percent. With three out of every four tribe members dead, cultural practices were threatened, including artistic traditions and the maintenance of long, complex oral histories.

The people of this dry, forbidding region were not easily conquered, however. They had sharpened their survival skills for centuries and were ferociously independent.

Keeping Tradition Alive

In spite of a history of attacks on their people and their institutions, some of the Native Americans in the Southwest have managed to sustain their lifestyles to this day through a careful balancing act. They have taken what they wanted from non-Indian culture, yet retained their own lan-

Native Americans keep their culture alive through their distinctive artwork.

guages and cultural traditions. Maintaining their cooperative ethic, the tribes have kept alive the lore of hunting, farming, healing, and ceremonial tradition. Their baskets, pottery, woven blankets, and other artistic works remain in high demand to the millions of tourists who today travel through the area. In addition, a new generation of southwestern Native American artists, musicians, and writers continue to produce beautiful and thought-provoking works that transcend time and culture.

At the dawn of a new millennium, the Native Americans' many contributions to southwestern culture remain strong and important. As Zdenek Salzmann and Joy M. Salzmann write in their guidebook, *Native Americans of the Southwest:*

Among the fifty states, New Mexico has the highest percentage of . . . Native Americans [who make] up about 9 percent of the state's total population. In Arizona the figures are . . . 6 percent for Native Americans. . . .

These groups keep alive their histories and their customs with colorful fiestas, pow-wows, religious ceremonies, historical celebrations and reenactments, and arts and crafts fairs that are full of vitality. Some of the distinctive crafts

Rainbow dancers proudly display their culture.

and art forms of the Native Americans are not only beautiful but also unique, not to be found elsewhere in the United States.[2]

It is because of such efforts of proud and dedicated groups of individuals that the background, cultural practices, and current lifestyles of the first peoples of the Southwest remain significant and meaningful contributions to the rich history of the Southwest—and the United States.

Chapter 1

Tribes of the Southwest

The rugged lands of the Southwest are unique and distinct, unlike any other land forms in North America. The elevations of different areas range from about one thousand feet to over thirteen thousand feet above sea level, and create many small regions with varying climates. These microclimates contain different plants and animals, and so influence the lifestyles of the Native American tribes in the region. The elevations, rainfall amounts, and temperatures in a region affect everything from the most basic food and shelter used by a tribe to the cultural and spiritual aspects of their religion.

In her 1929 book *The Rain-Makers,* anthropologist Mary Roberts Coolidge vividly describes the diverse physical features of the Southwest:

A fantastic region of color, contrast, and variability; dominated by high mountains, gashed by superb canyons, scarred with dry washes—the beds of intermittent streams—varied with immense shallow basins [and] rolling deserts . . . with bold buttes, flat-topped mesas, occasional forests and verdant valleys along infrequent water courses. . . . [A]nd everywhere are evidences of strange water and wind erosions and the marks of [ancient] volcanic upheavals, lava flows, hot springs, and extinct craters.

From mountain peaks of twelve thousand feet or more on the north, the mesa land, averaging six thousand [feet] elevation, drops beyond Salt River to the low desert along the Gila [River]. Inevitably there is a wide variety of climate—frost and heavy snows in winter on the higher levels, cool nights and hot days on the lower altitudes, and a long succession of days of dry and crystalline clearness. This clarity of atmosphere and the colorful quality of the landscape—where in places the rock, shales, sandstones, and clays show red, green, brown, blue, purple, yellow, and white—makes every detail stand out and distances very deceptive.[3]

The Land of the Southwest

To understand the tribes who have lived in the Southwest, it is important to understand the natural landscape and climate that make up the region.

The present-day state of Arizona is divided into several regions. In the north, the Colorado Plateau extends into four states that make up the Four Corners region (Utah, Colorado, Arizona, and New Mexico). Most of the elevations of this area are between five thousand and eight thousand feet. Outside of

The West Mitten butte in Monument Valley Navajo Tribal Park is part of the distinct landscape of the Southwest.

Flagstaff, Arizona, the highest point on the plateau is Humphreys Peak, which reaches the height of 12,633 feet. In this region, winter temperatures below freezing accompanied by several feet of snow are not unusual.

In his 1928 book *Under Turquoise Skies,* author Will H. Robinson describes the features of the Colorado Plateau:

> In the northern part of . . . Arizona, is the plateau country. Sometimes the land here is fairly level, at other times gently rolling, and all of it frequently cut through with washes, arroyos [deep, dry gullies] and small river beds. Some of these carry water only at times of storms, others have something of a stream in them through most of the rainy season, and still others are constant enough in this land of little rain to be classed as real rivers.[4]

A zone called the Mogollon Rim slants across Arizona from northwest to southeast and is composed of rugged peaks and spectacular red rock country as found around Sedona, Arizona.

The area known as the basin-and-range country lies south and west of the Mogollon Rim. The physical contours of this region consist of broad valleys, or basins, with elevations of two thousand to five thousand feet above sea level. The basins are sporadically interrupted by towering mountains that reach almost as high as eight thousand feet. The cactus-studded Sonoran Desert lies in this region as do the modern cities of Phoenix and Tucson where summer temperatures may reach as high as 120 degrees and daytime winter temperatures remain in the 70s and 80s.

The area is extremely dry, receiving only eight to twenty inches of precipitation annually. But, according to Coolidge, "the rain falls torrentially in violent brief thunderstorms; and where vegetation is meager . . . it turns dry washes into rivers for the moment, cutting channels through which the torrent disappears down canyons and into subterranean water levels."[5]

In the mountainous regions, however, twenty to thirty inches of precipitation a year is common, much of it in the form of snow. And although the climate is very dry, a variety of crops may be grown in the area. The Colorado River, the Rio Grande, and their tributaries, fed by the melting snows of the Rocky Mountains, allow for irrigation throughout the region.

In spite of these natural obstacles, Native American tribes in the region adapted to the harsh realities of the environment. Within nature's system, they developed balanced lifestyles and ways of spiritual sustenance whose traditions have lasted until this day.

The First Americans

Although it is commonly said that America was discovered by Christopher Columbus in 1492, North America was inhabited well before the fifteenth century by millions of people who were the ancestors of today's Native American tribes. These people are believed to have walked across the Bering Land Bridge—a landmass that emerged in the Bering Strait due to a drop in sea level during the Ice Age.

The Rio Grande River (pictured) contributes to the irrigation of the southwest.

Archaeologists believe that the first humans to enter the New World used the land bridge as they slowly migrated from what is now northeast Asia to northwestern North America between thirty thousand and twelve thousand years ago. The tribemembers followed the migration of big-game animals such as woolly mammoths, bison, camels, and giant sloths hunting the herds as they fed on the grass-lands in the region. As the Ice Age ended, the climate slowly changed to the arid conditions of modern times contributing to the extinction of the large mammals around nine thousand years ago.

The theory of the Bering Land Bridge, however, is often disputed by Native American tribes. According to Navajo tribesman Larry DiLucchio on the Navajo Central Website:

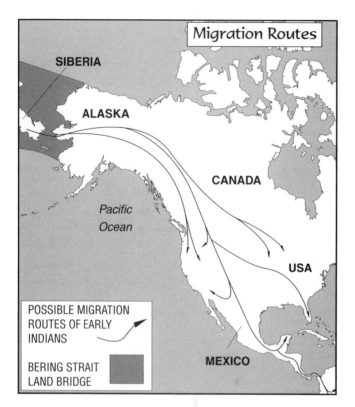

Migration Routes

SIBERIA

ALASKA

CANADA

Pacific
Ocean

USA

POSSIBLE MIGRATION
ROUTES OF EARLY
INDIANS

BERING STRAIT
LAND BRIDGE

MEXICO

ences. Until this is done, although their ideas may have merit, they will be discounted as unproven theories."[6]

Whatever theory one subscribes to, it is known that at the end of the Ice Age, after the big game had died out the tribes survived by hunting birds and smaller mammals such as deer, squirrels, rabbits, and rodents. To supplement their diets the tribes foraged for nuts, berries, seeds, and wild greens. Around five thousand years ago corn was probably carried into the Southwest by traders who traveled into what is now Mexico. Although corn, and later beans, were important staples in the tribal diet, they were not farmed but simply harvested in the wild. Hunting remained an important part of Native American survival. It was not until around 800 B.C., when people began systematically planting, weeding, and harvesting crops, that permanent settlements became possible. Then villages began to grow in the area, and from that time the number of people steadily increased.

The Tribe officially holds the Bering Strait theory to have been created and used by invading Europeans as a partial justification for the European's claim on North American lands and the westward expansion by people of the eastern states in the 1800s.

Some of the correspondents to DiLucchio's website, however, believe that the Navajo originated as far away as Tibet and the plains of Mongolia. These writers not only cite similarities between the languages, they also have genetic evidence to support their claims. Yet so far, DiLucchio continues, "they have not presented a step-by-step documented history of how this migration occurred, complete with refer-

The Early Tribes

Four major tribes with distinct cultural traditions slowly emerged in the Southwest: the Mogollon in southwestern New Mexico, the Hohokam of south-central Arizona, the Hakataya of western Arizona, and the Ancestral Pueblo peoples (sometimes called Anasazi) of northern New Mexico and Arizona. These tribes existed for a time and then mysteriously disappeared. Anthropologists suggest that a major drought might have caused the food and water supply to diminish to such a point that some people left their homes in response to the emergency and joined other tribes. Others may have chosen to stay and wait for rains, and when those did not come, they died of starvation.

The Mogollon culture, named after the Mogollon Mountains in southwestern New Mexico, began in the basin-and-range country of that region around A.D. 200 and lasted until about 1400. These people built secure villages in high locations, farmed, foraged, and hunted. They were among the earliest pottery makers and decorated their pitchers, jars, and bowls with animal figures such as fish, frogs, birds, and humans. They wore jewelry made of shell obtained through trade, played music on reed flutes, and hunted with darts, spears, and bows and arrows.

Land was not owned by individual persons, but shared by the community, a practice typical of Native American people. Archaeologist Edgar L. Hewett described this system in 1930 in *Ancient Life in the American Southwest*:

There was no individual ownership of land. Title was in the community, though heads of families enjoyed practically permanent tenure, conditioned upon a proper use of the land

and the performance of a fair share of the community work. Moreover, no community appropriated more land than was necessary to provide for immediate needs.[7]

The Hohokam lived in the Sonoran Desert around present-day Phoenix, and in a narrow region from the site of present-day Flagstaff in the north to the Mexican border in the south. Like the Mogollon culture, the Hohokam existed from about A.D. 200 to 1400. The Hohokam are widely known for having constructed canals that brought water from rivers as much as thirty miles away to irrigate crops such as corn, beans, and squash as well as cotton. (The modern canals that run through Phoenix and elsewhere in the region were constructed on the sites of ancient Hohokam canals.) Their dwellings were made of clay and straw and they fashioned high-quality pottery and ceramic figures. They made beads, mosaic plaques, bracelets, and pendants from shells obtained in the Gulf of California. Certain cultural aspects of the Hohokam, such as their ball games, lead anthropologists to believe that the tribe was once part of the Aztec or Mayan tribes further to the south in Mexico.

The Ancestral Pueblo people lived in the Colorado Plateau region north of the Hohokam and Mogollon people. These tribes have been known as the Anasazi for more than sixty years, but since Anasazi is a Navajo word meaning "enemy ancestors," Native Americans and

Cliff Dwellers

Beginning about fifteen hundred years ago, several tribes in the Southwest built dwellings directly into huge overhanging cliffs. These pueblos under their dramatic natural rock shelters represent the oldest identifiable human homes in the Southwest.

Today, people may still see these fascinating ruins in such places as Canyon de Chelly National Monument, established in 1931 on the Navajo Reservation in northeast Arizona. Here the sheer red sandstone walls of Canyon de Chelly and Canyon del Muerto rise to a height of about one thousand feet above the canyon floors. The ruins of numerous prehistoric cliff dwellings, the earliest of which date from the fourth century, are sheltered within these impressive cliffs. Ruins are also found within caves that extend deep into the canyon walls.

The most famous cliff dwellings in the park are the White House Pueblo, believed to have been occupied from about 1060 to 1275, and the Mummy Cave, dating from 1253. The Navajo themselves did not settle in the canyon region until about 1700.

No one knows why the ancient tribes abandoned their cliff dwellings. Some scholars suggest a long drought that severely reduced food supplies; others believe the threat of an enemy attack was sufficient to trigger a mass exodus.

The White House Pueblo pictured below is Canyon de Chelly National Monument's most famous cliff dwelling.

The Ancestral Pueblo people, who lived in northern Arizona and New Mexico, constructed groups of connected buildings called pueblos.

archaeologists now use the term Ancestral Pueblo.

The Ancestral Pueblo people lived in northern Arizona and New Mexico for more than three thousand years. They farmed corn and squash, hunted, and foraged wild plants and seeds. They were expert basket weavers who made trays, bowls, trunks, and water containers. The Ancestral Pueblo people learned to construct groups of connected buildings called pueblos ("pueblo" comes from Spanish, meaning "village" or "town") which were adjoining rectangular stone-and-adobe structures with several rooms. Between A.D. 900 and 1300, these villages grew in size and their inhabitants became accomplished craftspeople and artisans.

A less advanced culture, the Hakataya, inhabited the harsh Sonoran Desert region of west-central Arizona. The people practiced only marginal agriculture and relied on hunting and gathering to survive. They were nomadic, moving from place to place and living in disposable circular huts with thatched roofs.

The Pueblo People of Yesterday and Today

Whereas Native American tribes in regions, such as the East Coast of the United States suffered greatly when Europeans first arrived on American shores in the seventeenth century, many tribes in the Southwest were able to maintain their ancient cultures and traditions. Southwestern tribes also suffered from the activities of colonizers, but their rugged and remote location protected them for hundreds of years from the wars and near extinction experienced by tribes in other regions of North America. The website maintained by the Pueblo Cultural Center describes one such indigenous culture:

> Many centuries before European explorers found their way to the western hemisphere, the Pueblo Indians of what is now New Mexico developed a distinctive and complex civilization. These peace loving people created [a] . . . life in harmony with the environment and with each other. Their religion was pantheistic and deeply spiritual and constituted an important part of daily life, within which they created an equitable government, a magnificent architecture, intensive agriculture with a sophisticated irrigation system and a highly developed art in pottery, weaving, jewelry, leather work and other crafts.[8]

The Pueblo people of today are descendants of the prehistoric Ancestral Puebloans and the Mogollon people. Like their ancestors, they live in permanent villages. These villages are the Acoma, Cochiti, Isleta, Jemez, Laguna, Nambé, Picuris, Pojoaque, Sandia, San Felipe, San Ildefonso, San Juan, Santa Ana, Santa Clara, Santo Domingo, Taos, Tesuque, Zia, and Zuni Pueblos.

The Pueblos are divided into two groups. The western, or desert pueblos, in the mesa and canyon country of west-central New Mexico, consist of the Zuni, Acoma, Laguna and others. Also included in this tribal group are the inhabitants of the Hopi villages and one Tewa village of northeastern Arizona. The eastern, or river pueblos consist of more than a dozen different pueblos along the upper Rio Grande and its tributaries. These include Nambé, Taos, San Juan, Sandia, Zia, Jemez, and others.

All of these pueblos have interesting and varied histories. The Acoma Pueblo southeast of Grants, New Mexico, for instance, has been inhabited since before the twelfth century. Acoma means "People of the White Rock," and this pueblo is also called "Sky City" because of its location on top of a towering mesa, hundreds of feet above the surrounding countryside. The location was originally chosen for security purposes: marauding enemies would find it impossible to launch a surprise attack and prohibitively difficult to overcome defenders so well protected. There is little doubt, however, that the breathtaking view of the mesas and distant mountains also figured into the choice of the site.

The Hopi live in a dozen villages spread across three flat-topped rock monoliths known by outsiders as First, Second, and Third Mesas. The promontories lie in view of one another in northeastern Arizona, though First and Third Mesas are about fifteen miles apart. The Hopi land-

Hopi villages such as this one were often built on elevated terrain in order to provide protection from enemy attack.

holdings consist of about five hundred square miles of mesas and lowlands that lie entirely inside the much larger Navajo reservation. One of these settlements, Old Oraibi on Third Mesa, was established around A.D. 1100 and may be the oldest continuously inhabited site in the United States. (The Acoma Pueblo also makes this claim.) According to the Hopi Information Network on the World Wide Web:

The Hopi are unusual because unlike most other Native Americans, they have lived in the same place for nearly a thousand years. Possibly because they live so high up and far away from most other people, the Hopi, unlike most other Indians, were never forcibly moved from their homelands. Neither have they been targeted as systematically as other groups by missionaries seeking to convert Indians to Christianity. Consequently, the Hopi remain possibly the most culturally intact group of native people on the American continent.[9]

The Coming of the Apache

About one thousand years ago, small bands of nomadic tribes left their homeland in the barren, frozen regions of modern-day Canada and Alaska. They made their way south along the edge of the Rocky Mountains, following the bison herds on the western part of the Great Plains in the present-day states of Colorado and New Mexico. For several centuries, the immigrants moved ever southward, finally stopping in the southwest region. Upon their arrival the wanderers found the dazzling villages of the Pueblo tribes surrounded by acres of corn, beans, and squash.

One group of newcomers called themselves *Inde,* which translates to "the People." They became known as Apache because when they surrounded the Pueblo villages the Pueblo people identified them as *apacu,* meaning "stranger" or "enemy." The Spaniards later changed this word to Apache.

The bands of Apache who stayed near the pueblos adopted local customs such as making pottery, weaving, and farming. Other bands to the east took up the customs of tribes on the plains such as teepee building and buffalo hunting. For example, the Lipan Apache, who lived in the lower Rio Grande valley in New Mexico and Mexico, ranged towards Kansas when hunting buffalo. Other groups chose other paths. North of the Lipan, the Jicarilla Apache settled in northeastern New Mexico and southern Colorado, often hunting and camping along the Rio Grande near modern-day Santa Fe. The Mescalero band inhabited New Mexico from the Rio Grande to the Pecos River in southeastern New Mexico and often hunted in northern Mexico. Further south, where Arizona and New Mexico meet the Mexican border, the Chiricahua Apache made their homes. The final group was the Western Apache, who lived in southeast and central Arizona.

The Navajo

Although the Apache were divided into many subgroups, another part of this original group from Canada and Alaska became so different that they were no longer Apache. Like the Apache, with whom they had originally shared a language, the breakaway group also called themselves "the People": Diné in their language. "Navajo," the name most often used today, was first applied to the Diné by the Spaniards. Upon arrival in the Southwest, the Diné continued to develop their own distinct culture, settling in the country where the Ancestral Pueblo had lived in their magnificent cliff dwellings.

Since about 1500, the Navajo have lived side by side with the Pueblo people. During this period the Puebloan people influenced Navajo culture as farming techniques and other skills were passed from one tribe to the other. Always alert to the possibility of adopting useful components of other cul-

A Navajo elder recites an ancestral tale as skilled weavers make blankets.

tures, the Navajo also acquired livestock from the Spanish: horses, sheep, goats, and cattle.

Despite a long and sometimes unfavorable history of clashing with Spanish, Mexican, and American soldiers and settlers, the Navajo retain a significant portion of their ancestral territory, including lands they hold sacred in northeastern Arizona.

The Desert Tribes of Arizona

The far western edge of Arizona and northern Mexico is one of the hottest and driest deserts on earth with less than five inches of rainfall every year. In some years no rain falls at all. Small-leaved plants, cactus, and a few well-adapted animals manage to survive in this brutal climate. This area was also home to Native American tribes believed to be descendants of the ancient Hohokam peoples, who originally settled the more hospitable lands to the north.

The desert tribes are divided into two groups. The Pima and Papago lived along the Colorado River and its tributaries that flow into the Gulf of California. The Pima

Languages of the Southwest Tribes

The languages spoken by Native Americans in the Southwest fall into six linguistic groups. (A linguistic group consists of language families that are related, such as English and German.) These groups help anthropologists trace the origins of the tribes.

The Pueblo tribes represent four distinct linguistic groups, and members of those groups use numerous dialects. The Hopi, living in the semidesert of northeastern Arizona, speak a version of the Uto-Aztecan language shared by non-Pueblo tribes as widely separated as the Ute of Colorado and the ancient Aztecs of Mexico. Hopi villages separated by no more than a few miles have different dialects of this language family.

The Zuni, who live just across the border in New Mexico, speak a language related to the Penutian tongue spoken by California tribes. Seven pueblos, including the Acoma and Laguna, located east of the Zuni, speak a language known as Keresan, which is unrelated to any other Native American linguistic family. The remaining Pueblo peoples living along the Rio Grande derive their languages from the Tanoan family, which is divided into three distinct tongues known as Tiwa, Tewa, and Towa. In addition to their native languages most tribal members speak English and often Spanish as well.

The Apache, who probably arrived in the Southwest about five hundred to a thousand years ago, speak a version of the Athapaskan language. Other tribes who speak this tongue are the Inuit peoples, who live in Canada and the subarctic, and the Navajo.

originally called themselves "O'odham" or "the People" in their own language. They were called the Pima by the Spanish. The Papago called themselves the Tohono O'odham. When the Spaniards first came to the area, they counted around twelve thousand Tohono O'odham, whom they referred to as *papabotas* or "bean eaters," a term that was later shortened to Papago. In the 1980s, the Papago changed their name back to the Tohono O'odham. They are related to the Tepehuan and Tarahumara who occupy the steep canyons and rugged highlands of the Sierra Madres in Mexico. These tribes speak a language based on the Uto-Aztecan tongue of the former Aztec Empire in Mexico.

To the north of the Pima, along the Gila and Colorado Rivers, lived tribes such as the Yumans and Mohave, who spoke dialects of the Yuman language family. The Mohave lived upstream on the Colorado River near the desert that bears their name. This tribe came together with other tribes in the area in the nineteenth century to form the Maricopa tribe, who lived along the Gila River near the villages of the Pima.

The Pima, Tohono O'odham, and Maricopa tribes are related to the Havasupai and Yavapai in northwestern Arizona. The name Havasupai, which means "people of the blue-green water," refers to Cataract Creek, which empties into the Colorado River in the Grand Canyon. The Yavapai lived in the red rock mountains of Sedona, Arizona.

Ethnologists, who study the origins and characteristics of different groups of people, called the desert people who were seminomadic "village dwellers." They comprised one of three distinct groups of southwestern Native Americans. The numerous sedentary Pueblo peoples are referred to as the "pueblo dwellers," and the nomadic Apache and Navajo are called "camp dwellers." Each group has its own culture, religion, survival skills, and style of shelter. Together they make up a rich diversity of peoples, some of whom maintain their ancestral traditions in the modern age.

Chapter 2

Pueblos, Clans, and Family Life

Each Pueblo tribe lived in "a communal village of many-storied terraced buildings."[10] First devised to afford protection from nomadic tribes who traveled through the region in search of food and plunder, this form of architecture closely resembled the homes built by the Ancestral Pueblo people under the cliffs of Canyon de Chelly. To stave off the raiders the Pueblo tribes increasingly found themselves in need of walled cities to protect them from invasion. According to Anna Wilmarth Ickes in *Mesa Land:*

> The . . . pueblo people [from the sixteenth to nineteenth centuries] were in constant danger from marauding tribes. Ute, Apache, and Navajo swept down upon them, carrying off their crops and making prisoners of such workers as they surprised in the fields, and so the villages were designed for defense. Windows and doors faced the streets or the central court. Outside walls had no openings except for an occasional peephole, presenting forbidding blank walls to the surrounding country. Even these windows and doors existed only in the upper floors. The rooms on the lower tier opened only through a hatchway onto the roof and the roofs were reached by ladders which could be pulled up or, as can be seen still in some of the remote pueblos, the ladder had rungs stuck through the upright poles which could be pulled out. The entrance to the plaza, or the ends of the streets, could be quickly walled up with masonry.[11]

Pueblo villages of past centuries held about two hundred people. The homes were built up in tiers with each successive tier set back so that the roof of the room below served as a balcony for the room above. Families stacked dried food and firewood on the balconies and worked at various tasks including pottery-making, weaving, and cooking. When weather turned bad, the family moved into the twelve-foot by fourteen-foot rooms of their apartments, entered by a ladder that extended to a hatchway on the roof.

The Adobe Home

Pueblos may be divided into three classes. The pyramid pueblo is a large, square building terraced on all four sides. This results in pyramid-shaped buildings that narrowed at the top such as those of the Taos Pueblo, which rise to a height of up to six stories. The terraced pueblo, like those of the Zuni, were houses built upon one another, two or three stories high, with the roof of one forming the floor or the yard of the one above. Pueblos built in a tradition dating back thousands of years, such as those of the Jemez tribe, were arranged in a circle around an enclosed courtyard with a protective outer wall in the back.

Inside the honeycombed apartments of the pueblo, the floors were often paved with large, flat stones, and the small windows were covered with thin sheets of a mineral rock known as selenite that allowed

Ancestral Pueblo buildings, such as the White House (pictured), served as models for Pueblo tribes who wished to protect themselves from nomadic tribes.

light into the rooms. Most of the compartments were set aside for sleeping or food preparation, while dark rooms deep inside the complex stored food and clothing, precious stones, and other valuable items used for ceremonial purposes. The apartments were all connected to one another with interior doors so that in the event of an attack, people in the village could communicate with each other without stepping outdoors.

Another security feature was the door design: the doorways to the outside were very small, and for each one there was a large stone slab that could be moved in front of the door and held in place by strong poles.

In more recent times, the defensive intent of the pueblo was no longer important, so lower rooms were built with windows and doors. Upper tiers also disappeared, houses spread out, and some were even built as single-family detached dwellings. These trends have had the effect of largely eliminating a traditional way of indicating social status.

In *Zuni Indians,* written in 1904 for the Smithsonian Institution, Matilda Coxe Stevenson explains that a family's position in the tribe was indicated by which level they occupied in the community pueblo:

Among the Zunis . . . riches and social position confer importance upon the possessor. The wealthy class live in the lower houses; those of more modest means, next above; while the poorer families, as a rule, content themselves with the uppermost stories. No one, naturally, would climb to the garret who had the means to live below.[12]

Temporary Housing Allows Development of New Villages

In addition to their homes and villages, tribe members often worked and traveled far from the pueblo. In such cases temporary structures were built to store items and shield people from the harsh southwestern sun. The 1921 book *Indians of the Southwest* by ethnologist Pliny Earle Goddard describes how these shelters were built:

For the shelter of those who are tending the crops and as a camping place for the family when the fields are far from the village, temporary structures are built. The common type is made by setting four posts at the corners of a rectangle so that their forked tops are seven or eight feet above the ground. These posts support a platform of poles and brush which casts a shade and furnishes on its top a storage place away from dogs and stray animals. The Hopi often cut trees or brush and set them in curved or straight lines so as to break the wind and furnish the desired shade.[13]

When fields were very far from the main village, temporary rectangular houses of stone with flat roofs were built. As time passed, these farmhouses

Building a Pueblo

Men and women both participate in the construction of the pueblo. Men lay the stone foundations and build the walls from adobe—sun-dried bricks composed of earth and straw molded in wooden forms. After the adobe walls are built, huge logs that serve as support beams for the roof are laid on top. In this treeless region, logs of such size are a valuable commodity that must be brought from a long distance. After the logs are in place, carefully selected willow boughs are laid across the rafters. Sticks and brush are laid over this framework and the whole thing is covered with soil, forming a substantial roof.

After this part of the construction is finished, women cover the exterior walls with a reddish-brown plaster made from clay and water. The interior walls are made from white clay that is applied smoothly with a rabbit-skin glove. And, as Matilda Coxe Stevenson writes in *Zuni Indians:*

"The women delight in housebuilding, especially in plastering the houses. They consider this their special prerogative and

would feel that their rights were infringed upon were men to do it. . . . Little girls assist in bringing the water used in mixing the mortar, working industriously, and trudging from the river with their diminutive water vases on their heads."

When working the plaster, women keep their mouths filled with water which they skillfully sprinkle on the plaster to keep it malleable. The plaster protects the adobe bricks from the weather and may allow the buildings to last for centuries.

After men lay foundations and use adobe bricks to build pueblo walls, women cover the exterior walls with reddish-brown plaster.

In the past prosperous Zuni tribesmembers lived in the lower houses (pictured) while the poor settled in the uppermost dwellings.

might have multiplied until they became a village by themselves, with people only going back to the main pueblo for rituals and celebrations. In this manner, new pueblos formed across the region.

As new towns were added, even the sedentary tribes would abandon the old towns if a sufficiently pressing situation developed. Such a situation might be a spring drying up, enemies becoming troublesome, or a devastating epidemic sweeping through the village.

Semipermanent and Nomadic Shelters

The semisedentary tribes in the desert Southwest did not stay in one place long enough to construct elaborate apartment buildings. While the adobe houses of the pueblos were large enough for many families, tribes such as the Maricopa, Pima, and Tohono O'odham lived in one-family buildings grouped into semipermanent villages.

In the 1933 book, *Yuman Tribes of the Gila River,* Leslie Spier describes a typical Maricopa shelter:

> The Maricopa dwelling was dome-shaped, markedly flattened on top, and earth-covered. It was built on a central rectangular frame of posts linked by rafters, surrounded by a circular wall of poles bent over to be tied to the rafters, thatched, and dirt-covered. The construction was identical with that of the Pima and Papago and different from the earth-covered, but rectangular, hip-roofed houses of the Mohave and Yuma.[14]

Nomadic tribes such as the Navajo constructed simple shelters that could be abandoned with the change of seasons. In the winter, the Navajo lived in earth-covered lodges supported by three large logs with forked tops. These logs were locked together by placing the fork of one into the fork of the second and so on. Other logs and poles were piled on this framework until a pyramidal house was formed. Brush was placed between the larger cracks,

and a doorway was placed on the east side of the structure. Several inches of earth were piled on top of the entire structure, but a large hole was left at the apex to admit light and allow smoke to escape. These houses would not leak except during long, hard rains, which were rare in the Four Corners region. In the summer, the Navajo often camped under a shelter of brush or behind a small stone wall to protect them from prevailing winds.

In the winter, the Navajo constructed pyramidal houses by forking together logs and then filling in the large cracks with brush.

The Apache tribes west of the Rio Grande lived in frame huts covered with weeds or grass called wickiups.

The various nomadic bands of Apache did not show a great degree of uniformity in their structures. The eastern bands of the Apache lived in animal-skin teepees like those used by Plains tribes. All of the Apache tribes west of the Rio Grande made frame huts covered with weeds or grass called wickiups. These were constructed by placing saplings in a circle, bending them over to meet at the top, and lashing them together. Larger wickiups were built by forming a series of arches with the poles. A thatch, usually of bear grass, covered the frame and was held in place with strips of yucca leaves.

Clans and Family Organization

Like most other Native American groups in the United States, the Puebloan peoples are organized into extended families called clans. The peoples of the western pueblos generally trace their descent, hence their clan membership, through female tribe members. In this arrangement, called a matrilineal system, when a woman marries, her husband comes to live with her family. A woman's children, whether male or female, belong to her clan. If she has sons who become parents, each child belongs to his or her mother's clan.

Goddard offers additional details on the matrilineal system:

The young man, when accepted, comes to live with his wife's family. Later, his wife secures or builds for herself a new house or a set of rooms which adjoins her mother's. This house is her property and a dissatisfied husband in the case of separation leaves his wife in possession of the family home and returns to the house of his mother or sister.[15]

Each clan has its own name—derived from important natural features—through which it can be distinguished from the others. The pueblos were divided into many clans including Dogwood, Corn, Tansy Mustard, Pine, Firewood, Arrow, Eagle, Bear, Lizard, Cloud, Sun, Wood, Sky, Tobacco, and Turquoise.

Clan members may take turns as representatives in the pueblo government, in the administration of justice, and in the responsibility for traditional tribal ceremonies. Each clan owns particular magical objects (fetishes) and prayer sticks that are kept in the Clan Mother's household. As a result, that house becomes a social center for the clan.

Although descent is traced through a mother's clan, children also honor their father's clan. Stevenson writes about the child's role in the clan:

While descent [in the Zuni clan] is through the maternal side, the offspring is also closely allied to the father's clan. The child is always referred to as belonging to the mother's clan and as being the "child" of the father's clan. In the family the child is under the control of both parents. The clan plays an important part in ceremonials. Many ceremonial offices are filled either by a member of a given clan or by a "child" of the clan.[16]

As with some Pueblo peoples, the clan system is also very significant to the Western Apache bands and the Navajo. According to the Navajo Central Website:

The importance of one's clans is hard to over emphasize. Names one is called can and do change, but one's clans are forever. . . . In addition to . . . [the mother's] clan, Navajo people who have Navajo parents will have three additional clans; their father's clan and the clans of the mother's and father's father. These are used with the primary clan in determining relationships to others. Each individual must constantly fulfill different roles based on these relationships. A young woman may be a mother to some, sister to others, daughter or grandmother, all at the same time. Clan relationships are important. They can break down social walls, allowing an individual to be a distinct part of almost any group. Since other tribes also have clan systems, these relationships can also link tribes. The Coyote Pass People clan is common among the Navajo people, but it is said to have originated at the Jemez pueblo. On introduction to a new group of people, it is polite and expected to introduce oneself by clan membership first, then give your name. This provides an explanation of where you fit in the fabric of the society.[17]

Other Clan Systems

By contrast, the desert tribes divide their communities into groups called moieties, a system in which two population units make up a tribe. For instance, the Tohono O'odham are divided into two groups called the Red Ants and the White Ants. These groups, in turn, are further divided: The Red Ants are made up of the Akol, Apap, and Apuki; the White Ants of the Maam and Vaaf. These divisions play prominent roles in politics, ceremonies, and social games where one moiety competes against the other. Descent among the desert tribes is patrilineal—based on descent from the father's side.

Mary Roberts Coolidge sums up the importance of clan groupings and family descent as they influence everyday life among the different peoples of the pueblos:

Among the Hopi the clan distinction . . . is very important; while the easternmost pueblos lay much less stress upon it.

At some eastern pueblos it does not matter whether the bridegroom goes to his wife's house or she to his, but it is expected that he will ultimately provide a house. At Jemez three fourths of the houses are owned by men. . . .

But everywhere clan descent and the proprietorship of the family home go together. Thus, wherever the descent is traced from a maternal ancestor, the wife owns the home . . . so to speak. And where, as in some eastern villages, descent is in the paternal line, the man is proprietor of the family apartment. Among the western villages the women own the houses and the flocks and have at least an equal ownership of the crops and the standing harvest. The men . . . own the horses and cattle and have an equal ownership in the crops until they are stored in the house-granary.[18]

Marriage Customs of the Navajo and Apache

As in all other societies, life-changing events such as birth, marriage, and death are accompanied by important ceremonies. Before the twentieth century, marriages generally took place between the ages of fifteen and eighteen for a young man, when he became capable of hunting and supporting a family. A young woman would marry between the ages of fourteen and seventeen, when she was able to have children, grind corn, and maintain a household. In general, young girls were expected to remain virgins until they were married.

When a Navajo or Apache man wanted to marry a woman, he would try to impress her with his hunting skills. Thus the man came to a woman's lodge and laid a freshly killed deer outside. If the family was willing to have him as a son-in-law, the deer was taken in and eaten. The

In Apache tribes, a woman was not eligible for marriage until she was able to have children, grind corn, and maintain a household.

young man then lived with his father-in-law for some time while hunting to help support the family.

In ancient times, a strict mother-in-law taboo existed among the tribes: A young man was never allowed to be in the same room with or address his mother-in-law, her sisters, or her mother. If a man and his mother-in-law needed to communicate, a third person had to carry the message. The penalty for breaking this taboo was believed to be blindness inflicted by a supernatural power. No reason has been assigned to this taboo other than the strong feeling that it was improper for a man to know his wife's mother.

The Apache, whose survival depended on raiding the villages of other tribes, had different customs. A young Apache man had to accompany his father-in-law on four raids before he was deemed worthy of marriage. Among these tribes, marriage was considered less of a romantic venture than an economic arrangement. According to an unnamed Chiricahua Apache in *An Apache Life-Way:*

> Many of the old people think of marriage from an economic side. . . . I often hear people remarking that some boy has married just for love and wasn't sensible enough to take a girl who was a good worker and could provide a real home for him. . . .

Apache chief Geronimo had to prove himself worthy of his girlfriend by going on successful raids and providing her father with a herd of ponies.

If a man is industrious, he has more chance to get a match, and the same is true for girls. Some very ugly Indian

When a Child Is Born

Traditionally, when a Hopi baby is born the child's paternal grandmother makes four marks with corn meal on the four walls of the room. These marks are erased one by one on the fifth, tenth, fifteenth, and twentieth day of the baby's life. On each of these days, the mother and child have their heads washed with yucca suds. On the twentieth day, the grandmother washes the baby, puts corn meal to its lips, prays that the child will reach old age, and gives the child a name. Several women from the father's clan come at that time, bathe the baby and give it several more names. Pliny Earle Goddard explains the significance of the names in *Indians of the Southwest:*

"The names given relate in some way to the clan of the one who bestows them. Of the various names given the child, one, because it strikes the fancy of the family, generally sticks and becomes the child's name which is retained until the individual is initiated into some ceremony. This usually takes place between the ages of fifteen and eighteen."

After the child is named, the baby, mother, and grandmother travel to the eastern edge of the mesa, arriving around sunrise. They bring with them two ears of white corn that have been lying by the baby since it was born.

"The grandmother touches these ears of corn to the baby's breast and waves them toward the east. She also strews corn meal toward the sun, placing a little on the child's mouth. As she does this, she prays, uttering in the course of her prayer the various names which have been given to the child. The mother goes through a similar ceremony and utters a similar prayer."

men have gotten beautiful girls, not because the girls wanted them, but because the parents of the girl recognized their industry and insisted on the marriage.[19]

The famous Apache chief Geronimo went on several successful raids with his tribe. Afterward, he felt he proved himself enough to marry his girlfriend Alope.

Geronimo explained how he was married in his autobiography:

Perhaps the greatest joy for me was that I could marry the fair Alope, daughter of No-po-so. She was a slender, delicate girl. . . . I went to see her father concerning our marriage. Perhaps our love was of no interest to him; perhaps he wanted to keep Alope with him, for she was a dutiful daughter; at any rate he asked many ponies for her. I made no reply, but in a few days appeared before his wigwam with a herd of ponies and took with me Alope. This was all the marriage ceremony necessary in our tribe.[20]

Marriage Customs of the Puebloan Peoples

Among the Puebloan peoples, marriage decisions are left up to the individuals. When a young Hopi man has acquired some property and decides to marry, parents are informed. Marriages usually take place in the autumn or winter.

As recently as the 1920s, before a marriage could take place, a prospective mother-in-law would accompany her daughter to the young man's house with a tray of white cornmeal. She gave this to the young man's mother and returned to her house. The girl remained to grind cornmeal for three days. On the morning of the fourth day the relatives of the couple gathered at the fiancé's home. The mothers prepared bowls of yucca suds. Then the boy's mother washed the girl's head while the girl's mother washed the boy's head. Other female relatives rinsed the suds.

Goddard explains what happened next:

Zuni women transport pots of water. Woman also planted small gardens, tended to the children, and cooked meals for the family.

When the washing is finished, the bridal pair take a pinch of corn meal and walk silently to the eastern side of the mesa. They breathe upon the corn meal, throw it toward the rising sun, and utter a short prayer. When they have returned to the young man's house, the marriage itself is considered complete although the ceremony is not. The girl assists her mother-in-law in preparing a breakfast which is eaten by the members of both families. After the meal, the father of the young man runs out of the house and distributes bolls of cotton to the friends and relatives who are expected to separate the seeds from the cotton.[21]

A few days later, a town crier announced that the spinning of the cotton was about to commence. The male relatives of the couple gathered in the kiva, the pueblo's ceremonial rooms, and spent the day spinning cotton. At night they would bring the cotton to the bridegroom's house, where they would partake of a feast. The cotton was taken by the young man's father who, assisted by the other men, would weave it into two large white robes and a fringed belt. The men also would make a pair of moccasins with long deerskin strips. The robes and the moccasins were coated with white earth. This entire ceremonial process took six or seven weeks. After that time, the bride was dressed by the mother-in-law in the moccasins and one of the robes. The other robe was wrapped in a reed mat and taken by the bride to her mother. The couple then lived together with the girl's mother until a new home had been built.

Before and after marriage, daily life for Native American men and women involved long days of work. Women carried water, patched the adobe pueblos, planted small gardens, attended to the needs of their children, ground corn, and cooked. Men farmed the large corn and bean fields, and their day would begin with a run—often of many miles—to reach their crops. Other times there were rabbits to hunt and religious ceremonies to conduct. In this way, the people of the mesas lived out a stable and relatively peaceful existence for thousands of years.

Chapter 3

Seasons of Survival

Because of the vast differences in temperature and elevation in the southwest region, there is a great variety of vegetation.

A great variety of vegetation, including the cactus, can be found in the southwest regions.

In the mountainous regions over seven thousand feet, the hills are covered with Douglas fir, ponderosa pine, spruce, and aspen. Lower elevations favor juniper, Gambel oak, and piñon pine. In the Sonoran southwest, mesquite shrubs and creosote bushes are interspersed with fifty-foot-tall saguaro cacti, organ-pipe cacti, yucca plants, and Joshua trees.

Knowledge of Plants

Astute knowledge of southwestern plant life was an important part of Native American survival. To untrained observers the desert may seem like a barren wasteland. But to the Native Americans, plants such as the yucca provided dozens of uses. The roots yielded soap for the kitchen and bath, the fruit was used for a sweetener, and the leaves provided rope. The yucca was even used in religious rituals—the soapy lather represented clouds.

The leaves and roots of other southwestern plants were used for a number of purposes. Willow and sumac were used to

Native American women grind corn. In order to survive, Native Americans had to know how to sustain crops in the semiarid regions where the tribes lived.

weave baskets, hunting bows were made from chokecherry branches, and the hard mountain mahogany was used for hunting and war clubs. In addition, Pueblo and other southwestern tribes gathered dozens of types of leaves, roots, berries, seeds, nuts, and fungi. They harvested wild plants seasonally, picking wild onions in spring, harvesting the fruit of the prickly pear cactus in the summer, and gathering nuts from the cones of the piñon pine in the fall.

Food and Agriculture

Methods of securing and preparing food were central to the southwestern peoples' existence and also figured large in social life, religion, and art.

In the semiarid regions where the Pueblo tribes lived, farm fields were located by necessity along small streams and rivers. This meant that farm fields were sometimes located long distances from the pueblos—the fields of the Acoma, for instance, were fourteen miles from the tribe's village. The Hopi, however, located their fields closer to their mesas—anywhere there was a moist gulch or fresh spring.

Corn was planted by all the tribes in the region, but the Eastern Apache, the Jicarilla, and the Mescalero depended more on hunting than agriculture for their existence. The Apache also relied on wild food such as mesquite beans, prickly pear cactus, yucca fruit, and acorns.

The White Mountain Apache planted their crops in river beds while their neighbors, the Navajo, cultivated large fields in valleys that remained moist because they were shielded from the sun. The Pima and Tohono O'odham cultivated corn, beans, squash, cotton, and later wheat, which was introduced by the Spanish.

Unlike many other Native American tribes in North America, Puebloan men did most of the planting and harvesting. According to Goddard, writing in the 1920s, this was "because in the Southwest, agriculture is the chief means of securing food while in other regions it is of less importance than hunting and fishing to which the men principally devote themselves."[22]

To prepare a field, a gulch or sunken area was surrounded with a small earthen dam. When heavy rains came, the ground became saturated and soft enough to work. The corn was planted about twelve inches deep with a planting stick used to make a suitable hole. Instead of the long, straight rows seen today, the tribes planted their corn in clumps of eight or twelve plants.

After the corn was harvested it was dried by hanging it in long braids or spreading it in the sun on the roofs of the pueblos.

Chili peppers hang to dry next to a ladder.

Baking food in clay ovens was one Native American method for preparing meals.

The twisted braids were stored in cool back rooms of the lower stories of the buildings along with chili peppers, strips of dried squash, and dried meat.

The southwestern tribes inherited the food and farming techniques used by their ancient ancestors. In 1540, Pedro Castañeda, one of the first Spaniards in the region, described the Pueblo method of grinding corn, which had changed little over the centuries:

They keep the separate houses where they prepare the food for eating and where they grind the meal, very clean. . . . Three women go in here, each one having a stone, with which one of them breaks the corn, the next grinds it, and the third grinds it again. They take off their shoes, do up their hair, shake their clothes, and cover their heads before they enter. . . . A man sits at the door playing on a [flute] while they grind, moving the stones to the music and singing together. They grind a large quantity at one time, because they make all their bread of meal soaked in warm water, like wafers.[23]

For meals, native cooks were inventive and employed many methods of preparing corn including broiling, roasting, boiling, and baking in clay ovens. Green corn was roasted in holes in the ground that had been filled with live coals. Coolidge writes: "The teeth of the old people are worn almost to the gums with chewing the gritty corn and other hard food."[24] The corn was also made into cakes mixed with goat meat, mutton, jerky, or vegetables.

Hunting

Although farming and the harvesting of wild fruit provided most of the Puebloan peoples' vegetable-based diet, the men were also skillful hunters. Close to the pueblo, small mammals such as gophers, squirrels, and especially rabbits were hunted to fill the stew pot. Groups of men also traveled far from home to bring down antelope, deer, sheep, and other large animals. The Apache in the eastern regions often traveled to the Great Plains to hunt buffalo. And even the Hopi and the Zuni were known to make six-hundred-mile round-trips on foot to hunt buffalo.

Eating Cactus Fruit

Tribes such as the Pima and Tohono O'odham took advantage of the wild food that grew in abundance. The most esteemed food was the fruit of the giant saguaro cactus. The red buds of the cactus were gathered in early July, dried and pressed into small cakes consisting of the edible pulp. These cakes could be stored until they were needed; then they were boiled with water and eaten. The juice from the fresh saguaro was boiled and fermented into a wine that was the center of harvest festivals where men would drink the wine, sing songs, and dance.

Other tribes also used cacti as a food source. The fruit of the prickly pear cactus was gathered by women using tongs. The spines were rubbed off with a stone and the fruit was boiled, after which it was eaten with cornmeal porridge.

The Acoma tribe ate the roasted joints of the cholla cactus, which were sometimes split lengthwise, dried, and stored for winter food. The tribe also burned the spines off the pincushion cactus, which was eaten raw.

The fruit of the prickly pear cactus was a food source for some Native Americans.

Before horses were introduced to the region, hunting big game was a communal affair that involved driving animals into a dead-end canyon, a makeshift corral, or even deep snow. The trapped animals were then killed with bows and arrows or clubs. Rabbits were dispatched in this manner: Hunters would form a large circle in a field, walk toward the center, and kill their leaping prey by throwing sticks.

In 1912, anthropologist Carl Lumholtz described animals that were hunted by tribes in the Sonoran desert region of southern Arizona and Mexico:

An Apache attempts to obtain poison for his arrows from a rattlesnake.

In hot weather they followed jack-rabbits in the loose sand until the latter were exhausted. . . . They also killed mountain-sheep, which were not a difficult quarry, with their bows and arrows . . . and they were even able to approach mule-deer and antelope near enough to kill them by the same weapon. Lizards were eaten. At certain seasons they went to the [Baja] coast for the fishing, catching as many fish as they wished.

Lumholtz also noted that the skins of the animals hunted were used to fashion clothing:

The clothing of these people was made from the skin of mule-deer, antelope, or mountain-sheep. The hair was first removed with a bone taken from the lower foreleg of the animal, and the skin was smeared with the brains. The root of the torote tree, crushed and left in water, furnished necessary material for the tanning process. The man wore shirt and breech cloth, the woman a short skirt. . . . From the badger's hair they were able to plait ribbons for the hair and make twine to be used for the breech cloth.[25]

Apache hunters relied on their powerful bows and poison-tipped arrows for hunting. The poisons were concocted from blood and venom aged in the entrails of dead animals. These toxins were strong enough to kill a deer that had been merely grazed by such an arrow. During the lean winter months, Apache men raided the villages of other tribes, and later Spanish settlements. Women tanned hides, sewed clothing, made baskets, and tended the children.

The famous Native American warrior Geronimo wrote about Apache hunting practices in his 1904 autobiography:

> When I was about eight or ten years old I began to follow the chase, and to me this was never work. Out on the prairies, which ran up to our mountain homes, wandered herds of deer, antelope, elk, and buffalo, to be slaughtered when we needed them.
>
> Usually we hunted buffalo on horseback, killing them with arrows and spears. Their skins were used to make teepees and bedding; their flesh, to eat.
>
> It required more skill to hunt the deer than any other animal. . . . Frequently we would spend hours in stealing upon grazing deer. If they were in the open we would crawl long distances on the ground, keeping a weed or brush before us, so that our approach would not be noticed. Often we could kill several out of one herd before the others would run away. Their flesh was dried and packed in vessels, and

would keep in this condition for many months. The hide of the deer was soaked in water and ashes and the hair removed, and then the process of tanning continued until the buckskin was soft and pliable. Perhaps no other animal was more valuable to us than the deer.[26]

The Art of Living

While farming and hunting in the southwest region required a considerable amount of time and effort, the tribes spent countless hours integrating art into their everyday lives. The arts and crafts of the tribes consisted of making practical items that were also beautiful. Household items such as baskets, pottery, blankets, clothing, and moccasins were made with an attention to artistic quality unique to the southwest region. The Navajo specialized in weaving, silverwork, and basketry, while the Pueblo tribes were known for their pottery. The techniques for producing such items were developed dozens of centuries ago and remain in use today.

According to Navajo legend, supernatural creatures named Spider Woman and Spider Man taught the Diné to weave and to make looms. Anthropologists believe that Navajos knew how to weave when they came to the Southwest and learned new techniques from the Pueblo tribes. Whatever the case, Navajo blankets have been treasured for centuries, and Navajo tapestry methods continue to be respected today.

Navajo women weave their blankets from wool and color them with dyes from natural substances such as vegetables. As Zdenek Salzmann and Joy M. Salzmann write in *Native Americans of the Southwest:*

[V]egetable dyes made from various plants range through many shades of pastels: for example, soft brown from the bark of alder, light gray from the berries of ironwood, reddish purple from the roots of wild plum, bluish black from the leaves of sumac, tan from the blossoms of Indian paintbrush, light yellow from the flowers of wild celery, and so on.[27]

Weaving a Navajo blanket or rug is difficult and time-consuming work. It has

Weaving a rug is a difficult and time-consuming task requiring great artistry and skill.

been estimated that the production of a three-by-five-foot rug takes over four hundred hours, from shearing the sheep to spinning the yarn to working on the loom.

Basketwork

Basketwork is an art form even older than weaving—anthropologists believe

A three-by-five foot Navajo rug can take over four hundred hours to produce.

that Native American women in the Southwest have practiced this art for at least eight thousand years. Baskets served both ceremonial and practical functions and were basic necessities before clay pottery was made. In daily life, baskets were used as trays, bowls, jars, hats, hampers, and backpacks. Tightly woven baskets coated with piñon sap on the inside were even used to hold water. Decorations ranged from geometric designs to star and flower themes and animal representations.

Baskets have always been woven from plant material such as stems, leaves, or roots. The plants still in use today include willow, cottonwood, acacia, devil's claw, cattail, yucca, sumac, mountain mahogany, and others. The Salzmanns write, "Some plants are desirable for their natural colors used in the design—for example, from devil's claw, the black, and from yucca, mountain mahogany, and sumac, the reddish brown."[28]

Baskets are constructed from three types of weaving that date back to prehistoric times: wickerwork, coiling, and plaiting. Women of different tribes prefer different weaving techniques. The Jicarilla Apache, for example, are known for coiled baskets, while the San Juan Pueblo utilizes wickerwork. Tohono O'odham women weave something called a *kahau,* known as a burden basket, that consists of a basketwork body stretched across four dried cactus ribs. The *kahau* resembles a woven, framed backpack and is held in place by use of a headband.

Pottery

Pottery making is another ancient art, known to the Ancestral Pueblo people as early as A.D. 500. Early clay pots found in cliff dwellings were formed into simple shapes and painted with black designs. In later centuries, as the art developed, pots were painted with more complicated, artistic patterns. They were decorated with several colors and sometimes engraved with natural patterns of animals or plants. In the fourteenth century, Hopi potters began to paint black or red designs over an orange or yellow base.

Although men occasionally assisted in painting pieces, Puebloan potters were women. And the art was learned at an early age, with young girls working small bits of clay beside their mothers.

The Zuni specialty is a unique pottery style made from black clay. The black clay was and is obtained from the mesas near Ojo Caliente and Pascado. Stevenson writes: "The same clay is found in many localities, but so strictly do the Zunis adhere to custom that they could not be induced to use clay . . . from any other localities."[29]

Gathering the clay is considered a sacred act, performed by women in absolute silence and no men are allowed near the excavation site. At the turn of the century, one Zuni potter told Stevenson: "Should we talk, my pottery would crack in the baking, and unless I pray constantly the clay will not appear to me."[30] After gathering 150 pounds of clay in a blanket and positioning the burden on her back, each woman tied the blanket ends around her forehead and made the long journey back to the pueblo.

The only implements used in making pottery are the bottom of a discarded water vase and a trowel made from a gourd. Zdenek Salzmann and Joy M. Salzmann describe the Hopi pottery-making process:

[The potters] obtain the clay below the mesas, soak it, knead it, add grit (sand, [or] ground-up [fragments of broken pottery]) . . . and then mix it with water. Larger pieces are made by coiling—attaching a roll of clay to a flat round clay base and then coiling the roll spirally upward to the desired height. The curving, thinning, and smoothing of the walls is done with pieces of gourd and sandstone. After further smoothing with a pebble, the surface is covered with slip, a thin clay-based wash . . . and then decorated. Black pigment is generally obtained either by boiling tansy mustard leaves, pouring off the water, and squeezing the remaining pulp through cloth, or from black, fine-grained soft rocks ground and mixed with water. . . . For white, the potters use a fine white clay that they mix with water, and for yellow,

a clay containing iron hydroxide. Firing is done in the open, with dry sheep manure and occasionally native coal added to the wood fire. Temperature and length of firing must be carefully watched to prevent cracking, uneven or spotted coloring, or smudging.[31]

Although a discarded water vase and a trowel are the only tools needed to produce Native American pottery, the pottery-making process is complex.

The designs in the pottery are geometrical representations of mountains, clouds, and rainbows. Plants and animals, including the sunflower, the cotton plant, the parrot, and the turkey are also painted on pottery.

Turquoise Mining

While the artistic merit of household items such as pots and blankets was highly valued, none were held in greater esteem than the beautiful blue-green turquoise stones which permeated almost every aspect of Native American life. High-grade pieces were used for jewelry and those of lower quality were ground up into pigments or mixed with water to make magical potions. Many myths and legends surrounded turquoise, including one that said Pueblo gods had playthings, ornaments, weapons, and even houses made from the stone. Few festivals or rites took place without the official use of turquoise, and this meant that medicine men and shamans needed many pieces of this mystical mineral among their fetishes, amulets, and charms.

It is estimated that the use of turquoise goes back at least two thousand years. Its value to Native Americans is explained by Edna Mae Bennett in *Turquoise and the Indian:*

First, it was native to the arid region in which they lived, and it invariably occurred near the surface of the ground, which made it available and possible to get out of the ground with the primitive tools they had. Secondly, it was a soft and easily worked stone, colorful and attractive in very nearly its natural state. It had a lively color that contrasted with the garish colors of the land they lived in, while duplicating the color of things that they admired inordinately—sky and water. . . . The turquoise was never taken lightly; it was a positive influence for good, its good name was protected, and it has widespread use by the Indians of the Southwest even today.[32]

Adding to its mystique, the turquoise stone is found in a wide variety of colors including sky blue, greenish blue, dark blue, dark green, reddish brown, white, and even violet. Some Native Americans were able to recognize up to two hundred different colors in the stone.

Although the Spanish who came to the region in the 1500s were not at all impressed with turquoise—they were looking for gold—they mentioned the stone in their journals. In 1536, a priest named Marcos de Niza wrote, "[The Indians] part their hair on the side with a number of twists exposing their ears, from which they hang many turquoises, as well as from their necks, wrists and arms."[33]

When the conquistadors arrived in North America, Native Americans had over two hundred turquoise mines in the region. Since digging in the sharp, hard rock of the Southwest was a time-consuming and laborious process, most turquoise mines were simply saucer-shaped depressions fifteen to thirty feet across and half as deep. Some more sophisticated mines had long vertical shafts, horizontal entrances to the mine, or tunnels and rooms dug into a hillside. Pillars were propped up in the mines to support the roofs and tunnels.

In 1881, science writer Benjamin Silliman marveled over the work that went into digging out the ancient turquoise mine at Cerrillos near Santa Fe:

The whole north side of the hill has been quarried, and other working has been done on the other sides of the hill. It seems incredible that such a mass of rock could be moved by a primitive people without any modern appliances. The excavation is 200 to 300 feet in width. This excavation is made in solid rock, and thousands of tons of rock have been taken out. Debris covers 20 acres. On the sides

The Turquoise Road

Turquoise has been mined in Pueblo country for more than two thousand years, and the beads and jewelry left behind are used by archaeologists as clues to ancient trade routes. A fourteen-foot-long necklace of stone beads, with three large chunks of turquoise, was found in a wall in the ruins of an Ancestral Pueblo town of Chetro Ketl, at the great complex of abandoned towns in Chaco Canyon, New Mexico, now a national park. The turquoise in the necklace came from a huge underground mine at Cerrillos, New Mexico, that was at the center of nine turquoise-trading pueblos and dozens of outlying villages that grew into a large civilization in the region around A.D. 700.

Eventually hundreds of miles of "turquoise roads"—covering more than one hundred thousand square miles—crossed the region. The roads allowed people from small farming villages to travel to annual trade fairs and spiritual ceremonies, where they gladly traded their surplus food and other goods for the valuable turquoise, which played an important role in religious ceremonies.

By A.D. 900, the region thrived with major trade taking place south over the Sierra Madres, via the turquoise road, to the Toltec Indian capital north of Lake Texcoco in Mexico. Because of this demand for turquoise, the blue-green stone served as money and was the basis of wealth for the Ancestral Pueblo civilization.

The ancient Pueblo civilization coveted turquoise and used the blue-green stone as currency.

and slopes are growing cedars and pines over 100 years old. Many stone hammers and implements are [also to be] found.[34]

The turquoise stone was wrenched from the ground with stone hammers, picks, and mauls attached to wooden handles by leather straps. The ore was carried out in animal-skin buckets or reed burden baskets. Fire was used to crack apart the rocks that surrounded the turquoise, and the final remnants of stone were chipped away from the remaining gem with implements of deer horn, elk horn, or tortoise shell.

Although digging turquoise stone was difficult work, the stone was infused with

Native Americans of the Southwest used stone hammers, picks, and mauls to extricate turquoise stone from the ground.

a religious and magical significance and found an important use in the spiritual and healing rituals conducted almost every day in the pueblos of the Southwest.

Chapter 4

Spirits and Healing

The spiritual and religious practices of the southwestern tribes are incredibly numerous, very intricate, and are different in each tribe. There is one basic belief, however, that the tribes hold in common: They recognize humankind's oneness with the universe and maintain harmony and balance through the correct execution of religious rituals. This philosophy is summarized in practical terms in *Southwestern Indian Ceremonials* by Tom Bahti: "If the ceremonies are properly performed, the rains will fall, harvests will be bountiful, the life of the people will be long and happy, and the fertility of the plant and animal world will continue."[35]

Every aspect of Native American life and death is infused with spiritual importance and mythical significance. And the tribes hold a very definite idea about the world in which they live. The Tewa Hopi know the world as *'opa,* believe it to be alive, and worship it as "Universe Man." The Keres of Santa Ana believe they understand the nature and shape of the uni-

verse; this entails knowing all the gods, goddesses, and spirits, where they live, and what they do to affect humanity.

At the Santa Clara Pueblo, the earth is considered to be the center of the universe, while the sun, moon, stars, and planets exist to make the earth habitable for human beings. The earth is called "Our Mother" and in the ancient tradition was represented as a flat square with each corner having its own name. In early Jemez depictions, the earth is seen as flat but round, like a pancake. The Zia developed a cosmic picture in which the universe is made up of three parts: the earth, the middle plane, and the upper plane, each inhabited by its own deities and spirits.

According to traditional Tewa belief, there is a world inside the earth where a pale moonlike sun shines at night. Long ago, the Tewa emerged from this underground and were taught by gods called kachinas how to farm, hunt, organize their society, and preserve good relations with the universe. It is believed that when the sun sets in the west it passes through a lake and into this world below the surface, contuing its path until it comes up in the east the next morning. The sky is personified as "Sky Old Man," who is the husband of "Earth Old Woman." (The terms "old man" and "old woman" are used by the Tewa with the deepest reverence.) The children of the old man and old woman are the Tewa themselves.

The Pueblo people regard certain mountains as sacred homes to gods, goddesses, and spirits whose powers often include control of the weather. The Tewa say that the wind comes from Sandia Mountain, where Old Woman Wind lives. The Acoma speak of deities in the surrounding mountains who bring different types of precipitation—drizzle, rain, mist, and snow. The Tewa look to a particular mountain to predict the kind of weather they will have. In addition, native people make their way to revered mountains to gather sacred objects such as eagle feathers, evergreens, and paint pigments used in rituals.

Pueblo Rituals and Ceremonies

Pueblo tribes—and all of the tribes of the Southwest—celebrate their religion

Pueblo people believe that through rituals and dance they can influence the actions of invisible supernatural forces that control nature.

with rituals that serve to nourish the spirit, heal the sick, and provide occasions for joyous social gatherings. Because the ancient tribes had no written language, the retelling of tales during ceremonies is also an important way to keep beliefs, stories, and traditions alive year after year. The ceremonies take the form of dramatic plays in which the movements and activities of supernatural spirits and animals are acted out. The actors paint their bodies, wear masks, and imitate the moves and appearance of the characters they are representing. Deities are also depicted in these ceremonies by large stone images and smaller dolls carved from wood or stone.

The tribes keep permanent shrines to their deities near their villages. These shrines are often surrounded on three sides by walls of stone. When it is time to perform a ceremony, sacred sand paintings are made in front of temporary altars which have been constructed specifically for the observance. These dry sand paintings are made by sprinkling colored sand to form pictures and symbols of gods.

Goddard summarizes other common Pueblo religious practices:

Small sticks, singly or in pairs, are painted and often have faces indicated on them. Feathers, and a corn husk containing corn meal and honey are usually attached to them. They are placed at the shrines and springs for the deities. Corn meal and pollen are strewed and thrown

Native Americans depend on ceremonies such as the Eagle Dance (pictured) to keep their beliefs, legends, and traditions alive.

toward the sun. Corn meal is also frequently used to mark ceremonial trails and to define the limits of sacred places. . . . Bathing the head and the use of [substances that cause vomiting] are resorted to as methods of purification.[36]

In general, most southwestern ceremonials use dramatic rituals and pictorial art to influence invisible supernatural powers and through them, natural forces. A great number of ceremonies are performed to bring rain and to aid growing crops.

Mystical Societies

To maintain their spiritual beliefs, the Pueblo tribes organize themselves into voluntary societies that recruit young people, train them in secret lore, and perform special duties. These societies are charged with carrying out various activities in the physical and mystical world that are vital to the community. Some societies, for instance, specialize in hunting, hunting rituals, and hunting traditions. Others are concerned with the important phases of agriculture. These individual groups perform ceremonies to bring rain, promote growth of crops, and insure a good harvest. In the centuries before the federally administered reservations system existed, the policing of the village was overseen by one voluntary society and the power to wage war was held by another.

In 1630, a friar named Alonzo de Benavidez wrote the book *Memorial* in which he attempted to describe the initiation process for one of these societies—the Bow Society of the Zuni:

> To make one a [member of the society] they used to come together in a plaza and tie him naked to a pillar, and with some cruel thistles they all flogged him, and they afterward entertained him with farces and other jestings. And if to all he was very unruffled and did not weep nor make grimaces at the one nor laugh at the other, they confirmed him for a valiant captain.[37]

The work of the societies was holy, and the sacred knowledge was passed along from generation to generation. Each organization was headed by a priest who held that position for life.

Kivas

In all pueblos ancient and modern, certain ceremonial rooms are constructed specifically for use in sacred rituals. These rooms, called kivas, form the heart of each pueblo. Since Pueblo legends state that in past ages the people emerged from underground, kivas are always built at least partially underground. In *The Pueblo Indian World,* Edgar L. Hewett and Bertha P. Dutton describe conventions associated with the use of kivas:

> In olden days, Pueblo men gathered in the kivas to practice and prepare for ceremonials; to make prayers, offerings, and sacrifices; to engage in

conferences; and to do their weaving and other manly pursuits. Early Spanish accounts tell that the young men lived in the kivas and that women were forbidden to sleep in the kivas, or to enter them except to give food to their menfolk. This is not always the case; in some pueblos women go in and out freely in preparing for and participating in the ceremonies. It may be said that the kivas belong to the men, the houses to the women. Their general use is about the same today as in the past.[38]

Each village has several kivas which contain altars decorated with paintings of clouds, corn, lightning, and other sacred objects. Inside the kiva there is praying, singing, and dancing. The ritual smoking of sacred tobacco is another kiva activity, one that is considered to be very important because the smoke is believed to attract rain clouds.

Ceremonial rooms called kivas (pictured) are built at least partially underground and are used in sacred rituals.

Kivas are decorated with murals such as this one which depicts a figure with lightning and rain.

Hopi Kachina Season

For tribes such as the Hopi, life is steeped in ritual. The solar year is marked by a succession of ceremonies used to insure harmony with the universe and the safety and health of tribe members. The ceremonial year is divided into two halves. The most intense activity begins on the winter solstice around December 21 and ends in mid-July. This time of the ceremonial year is called kachina season after the masked performers who dress as kachinas, the spir-its who taught the Hopi how to live on earth. Major ceremonies last anywhere from four to twenty days, but only the last day or two of each ceremony is held in public outside the kiva.

About three hundred different kachinas are represented in ceremonies. Their masks and costumes portray wild plants, foods, aspects of weather, birds, and other animals. Only men can wear the masks, and they must be trained and indoctrinated into the sacred ways before being allowed to participate in a ceremony. The

Kachina Dolls

The Hopi call their gods kachinas, which are personified in human form by masked kachina dancers. These dancers, in turn, are represented by wooden kachina dolls, that have been carved by Hopi artisans for hundreds of years. During tribal ceremonies, the kachina dancers hand out the dolls to children who have gathered for the ritual.

The dolls, which are eight to twenty-four inches in height, are modeled after the costumes of the dancers and, like the dancers, hold drums, rattles, or bows and arrows. Zdenek Salzmann and Joy M. Salzmann explain how kachina artwork has evolved, and the signficance of dolls in *Native Americans of the Southwest:*

In traditional kachina dolls, color indicates which of the six cardinal directions the [kachina] has come from. Yellow stands for the north or northwest, blue-green for the west or southwest, red for the south or southeast, white for the east or northeast, black for zenith or above, and nadir, or below is multicolor. The color of the doll's head and body also indicates whether the spirit represented is benevolent or evil."

Since World War II, kachina dolls have become valued by non-Native Americans and their worth has increased. Today, carving and selling kachinas is a good source of income for Hopi craftsmen.

"Cottonwood root is used because it is the respected traditional material, is light in weight, can be easily carved, and does not easily dent....

For the painting process, mineral and vegetable dyes were used on early kachina dolls. During the twentieth century, carvers have used poster paints . . . [and] acrylics. In addition to paint, the dolls are often embellished with shells, leather, fur, painted cloth, wool yarn, bits of silver, and feathers....

Kachina dolls are designed to look like Kachina dancers and are handed out to children during tribal ceremonies.

masks are believed to transform the wearer, giving him the supernatural powers of the spirit he is impersonating. In this costume, he dances privately in the kiva and later in the town plaza.

On the winter solstice, the kachina named Soyal arrives and opens the kivas so that the other masked dancers may appear. This is the Hopi New Year, and it is marked by depositing offers to the gods such as smoothed sticks, feathers, string, grass, and other materials that are regarded as symbols of prayers. In the months following New Year, many more kachinas arrive, sometimes bringing gifts for children such as kachina dolls for the girls and bows and arrows for the boys.

During this time, when there is little work to be done in the fields, secret societies may spend weeks in their individual kivas. Then, in the spring, the entire village is swept up in public dances to prepare for the planting. The kachinas concentrate on bringing rain and promoting the fertility of the earth. Finally in July, when the first corn is ripe, the kachina called Niman arrives and sends the kachinas back to their underworld home where they will stay until the next December.

Although these spiritual duties are very serious, tradition also holds a place for humor, and the rituals are attended by clown kachinas. On ceremonial days, clown kachinas—painted with black-and-white stripes—enter the village plaza by clamoring over rooftops, all the while stumbling and tripping on their way to the plaza. Once in the plaza, they irreverently throw cornmeal at the dancers and shout rude questions. The clowns interact with one another, squabbling over morsels of food, calling to each other in loud, harsh tones, and mocking the rules of social behavior that govern everyday life in the normally restrained Hopi society.

During breaks in formal ceremonies, clown kachinas mimic the dancers while employing lewd gestures. The assembled crowds roar in laughter as the clowns ridicule everyone from schoolteachers to camera-laden tourists assembled for the ceremony.

Although the Pueblo peoples have highly intricate and evolved religious beliefs, other tribes in the region are also known for their spiritual practices.

Spiritual Beliefs of the Nomadic Tribes

Like the Pueblo, the Apache honor sacred spirits and natural phenomena, and spiritual life is inseparable from daily routine. To honor and influence the gods, the Apache have observed dozens of rituals and taboos whether they were planting corn, gathering saguaro fruit, or raiding a Spanish village. While hoeing the fields, the Apache addressed the corn seeds, which were thought to contain the sacred power of the universe. Unlike the Pueblo people, who honored lightning,

Apache people feared lightning and would never plant their crops in a field where it had struck. A person who had survived a lightning strike was not allowed to help plant crops. After crops were planted, Apache shamans placed sacred feathers in the fields to lure rainfall.

Before beginning a hunt, an Apache man purified himself with a sweat bath and avoided eating meat and salt. The night before a hunt, the men sang, prayed, and offered sacrifices to the spirits. While on the chase, hunters would offer puffs of tobacco smoke to the sun before stalking their

Apache men purified themselves in a sweat house (pictured) before beginning a hunt.

quarry. Each kill was performed in a ritualized manner and hunters avoided game whose meat was taboo such as coyotes, wolves, and foxes.

Geronimo wrote about Apache religious life in the nineteenth century:

> We had no religious organizations, no sabbath day, no holidays, and yet we worshiped. Sometimes the whole tribe would assemble to sing and pray; sometimes a smaller number, perhaps only two or three. The songs had a few words, but were not formal. The singer would occasionally put in such words as he wished instead of the usual tone sound.

> Sometimes we prayed in silence; sometimes each one prayed aloud; sometimes an aged person prayed for all of us. At other times one would rise and speak to us of our duties to each other and to Usen [the Great Spirit]. Our services were short.

> When disease or pestilence abounded we were assembled and questioned by our leaders to ascertain what evil we had done, and how Usen could be satisfied. . . .

> If an Apache had allowed his aged parents to suffer for food or shelter, if he had neglected or abused the sick, if he had profaned our religion, or had been unfaithful, he might be banished from the tribe.[39]

Like their Apache neighbors, the Navajo lived in a world animated by supernatural beings who needed to be constantly mollified through ritual and taboo. The Navajo conducted elaborate ceremonies that lasted up to seven days that included chants, performances by sacred singers, and the construction of sand paintings that recounted intricate legends of the tribe. By performing these rituals and behaving properly in their daily lives, the Navajo sought to maintain an ideal state of balance in the universe.

Sky Watchers

Tribes of the Southwest consider themselves to be the offspring of Mother Earth and Father Sky. From this perspective, the stars are not thought of as remote and distant objects but as windows on the cosmos and instruments for understanding the world. In his book *Archaeoastronomy,* historian Ron McCoy explores the significance of the stars to the southwest tribes:

> In the Four Corners region . . . Indian peoples have been gazing at the sky for countless generations, ingeniously applying its signs to their daily lives. We see evidence of their interest everywhere. Scattered across the Four Corners are rocky outcrops painted and pecked with designs that receive direct sunlight

Sand Painting

The ancient art of painting with colored sand was chiefly practiced by the Hopi and the Navajo and used for spiritual and healing ceremonies. The technique for making a large painting was described by nineteenth-century author Washington Matthews and reprinted in *The Rain-Makers.*

"Some of [the Navajos'] larger pictures, in their great nine day ceremonies, are ten or twelve feet in diameter, and represent . . . various gods of their mythology, divine ceremonies, lightning, sunbeams, rainbows, mountains, animals and plants, having a mythic or traditional significance. . . . [I]n order to prepare a groundwork for a sacred picture in the lodge, several young men collect, with ceremonial observances, a quantity of dry sand, which is . . . [spread] on the floor of the lodge. . . .

The pigments represent the five sacred colors of Navajo mythology—white, blue, yellow, black and red. . . . [T]he white, yellow and red are made of finely powdered sandstone . . . the black of powdered charcoal . . . and the blue (really gray) of black and white mixed. . . . To apply the pigments the artist picks up a small quantity between his first and second fingers and his opposed thumb and allows it to flow slowly as he moves his hand. . . . The drawings are begun as near the center as the design will permit . . . and according to an exact system. . . . The naked bodies of the gods are first drawn and then the clothing is put on. . . .

When [the sand painting] is finished, ceremonies are performed over it, and then with song and ceremony it is obliterated. . . . The Navajo make and destroy a picture on one day."

A Navajo child sits in the center of a sand painting during a tribal ceremony.

only at certain cosmically significant times. Ceremonial chambers called kivas at the great prehistoric center of Chaco Canyon, New Mexico, appear to be constructed so that specific areas are illuminated only on key days of the celestial year. Around northeastern Arizona's Canyon de Chelly, stone ceilings in caves and under remote outcrops are decorated lavishly with paintings of stars. All of these phenomena speak of the close attention the heavens command, and all are of interest to archaeoastronomers—those who specialize in the study of ancient astronomical practices.[40]

The Navajo tell of how Black God made the stars by stomping his foot to remove the seven stars of the Pleiades constellation from his ankle. He then reached into his pouch and removed a single, shining crystal which he carefully positioned in the sky to become the North Star. Black God received help from First Man, who skillfully arranged Revolving Male (Ursa Major), and from First Woman, who assembled Revolving Female (Ursa Minor). Other constellations soon joined the revolving pair in the sky.

The mischievous trickster Coyote got involved. Coyote felt that Black God was taking too long to fill the sky with stars, so Coyote took the deity's pouch and flung its contents across the sky. This is why some stars have names and are arranged in neat constellations and others are nameless and randomly scattered.

The stars remain sacred to southwestern tribes even today. Pueblo astronomer-priests called Sun Chiefs treat sky watching as a solemn religious duty, marking the location of the rising sun every morning. McCoy explains the reason:

These people are farmers. . . . Dependence upon sun, rain, soil, and seed for sustenance imposes a need for accuracy in any observations establishing the best times for planting and harvesting crops. All of this is directly related to the arrival and departure of warm and cold weather. Thus, their knowledge that the equinoxes and solstices mark the seasons' arrivals and departures may be the most valuable information they possess.[41]

In Hopi villages the observations of a Sun Chief help establish the proper time for important rituals, including the winter solstice ceremony (around December 21, the shortest day of the year), and various harvesting and planting rituals. It is also around the time of the winter and summer solstices that the Pueblo villages conduct relay races intended to influence the sun's movement.

Medicine Men

All tribal systems of the southwest region, and indeed all Native American tribes, give prominence to a person known as a medi-

A medicine man attempts to heal his patient. Relieving physical suffering is one of the many duties of a medicine man.

cine man, or shaman. This position requires a lifetime of training and the duties of the shaman are difficult. He is called upon by tribe members to consult with the deities and is expected to relate the desires of the gods to the people. He is also asked to relieve physical and spiritual suffering, to pre-

side over ceremonies, and to train young men in the ways of the shaman.

The medicine man is expected to devote his life to fasting and prayer. The fasts may last from one to four days according to the seriousness of the peoples' need. Because he is believed to speak for the gods, his influence over tribal affairs is very great. He is not supposed to intervene in petty discussions or mundane affairs, and his wants are provided for by the people who supply him with wood and cultivate a field for his benefit.

Among the Pima and the Tohono O'odham, there are two classes of shamans. The *Makai,* generally men, deal with the weather and crops. The *Siatcokam,* who cure sickness, usually inherit the positions, and both men and women are eligible. And, as Goddard states, "the novices who wish to become priests of this sort undergo a training lasting from two to four years."[42]

Shamans rely heavily on the power of visions as seen in dreams. In *Apache Life-Way,* an unnamed shaman relates that he has been guided his entire life by dreams, and that dreams have helped him fight against sickness and danger:

The dreams always come unawares, and, whenever there is danger ahead, I dream a warning. Whenever someone is sick, I dream of what plant to use as medicine. In case of danger I [would] see the enemy leader face to face, and he would tell me when the battle was to occur. In sickness I would actually see the plants to use. All my dreams have come true. I consider myself lucky and ascribe my present [old] age to dream help. I have been in many battles, but my dreams have told me what to do, and so I have never been wounded. I tell my close friends about my dreams and help

them too. I must be a shaman or I couldn't dream this way.[43]

Tribal members of the Southwest believe that most disease is caused by witches or the spirits of animals that have been mistreated. The Tohono O'odham believe that rattlesnakes cause stomach problems, offended turtles can cripple a leg, and an injured deer can afflict its tormentor with rheumatism.

Although ceremonies and ritual play a large part in healing, Native Americans possess a wide knowledge of herbs and plants with proven healing abilities. Stevenson writes about Zuni medical practices in the early twentieth century.

Though the [medical] practice of the Zunis is to a large extent [based on ritual magic], it is rich in legitimate [herbal] drugs. Some of these drugs are employed in conjunction with [religious ceremony]; but frequently medicines are administered . . . in the most matter-of-fact way without prayers or incantations, not only by old women, who know various plant medicines, but also by the . . . man or woman who is always a [shaman] of some esoteric fraternity. . . .

While these medicines, which are mainly plants, are used in conjunction with fetishes . . . they are generally of real medicinal value. Massage is extensively practiced, and the masseur or masseuse is most proficient.[44]

The healing abilities and elaborate spiritual beliefs practiced by the southwestern tribes evolved over many centuries. Very few Native Americans ever doubted these basic truths or called them into question. It was another matter, however, when the Spanish arrived in the seventeenth century and began to preach a new set of religious beliefs that the natives were expected to obey without question. From that time forward, many of the tribes of the region either modified their practices to fit with Christianity, or continued to practice their ancestral religion in secret.

Chapter 5

Clash of Cultures

Christopher Columbus sailed his ships from Spain to the Caribbean in 1492 looking for a trade route to India. Soon dozens of other European explorers followed in his wake. On the morning of April 21, 1519, six hundred Spanish soldiers led by Hernán Cortés landed on the eastern coast of Mexico near the modern-day city of Veracruz. This territory was part of the Aztec Empire. The Aztecs were relatives of the Pima and Tohono O'odham in Arizona.

Cortés and his men quickly marched to the Aztec capital of Tenochtitlán, which was filled with awe-inspiring art and architecture. When the Spanish soldiers reached the city they were astounded by the wealth of gold, silver, and precious jewels found there. Bernal Díaz del Castillo, a writer brought by Cortes to record the invasion, described it, saying: "With such wonderful sights to gaze on, we did not know what to say, or if what we saw before our eyes was real."[45]

Within two years Cortés and his men had reduced Tenochtitlán to rubble. An

European explorers such as Francisco Vazquez de Coronado (pictured) sailed to Mexico in the sixteenth century.

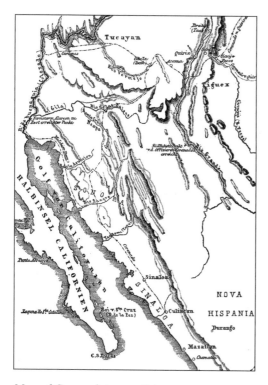

Map of Coronado's expedition.

The Spanish found no cities of gold; instead, according to the expedition's chronicler, they found "a little crowded village."[46] For their part, the Pueblo people must have been deeply startled by the horse-mounted, armor-clad soldiers wielding death-dealing muskets and trailed by cavalcades of cows, sheep, and goats.

Spanish Clash with the Pueblo People

Coronado first arrived at a Zuni village on July 7, 1540. After some intense fighting in which Coronado was wounded, the Pueblo people retreated to the heights of Thunder Mountain, leaving their village to the Spanish. Using the Zuni village as a base, various parties of soldiers fanned out across the region. A few visited Hopi villages, and several marched past the "Sky City" of the Acoma Pueblo. Coronado's men spent the winter in a Pueblo village on the Rio Grande near Bernalillo. But, according to Goddard:

estimated one hundred thousand natives were killed in bloody battles as the Spanish systematically looted the Aztec Empire. By 1525 hundreds of ships, called galleons, were returning to Spain overloaded with plundered Aztec treasure. The land the Aztecs had inhabited for generations was renamed New Spain.

In 1540 Spanish soldiers led by Francisco Vazquez de Coronado marched north from New Spain to the land of the Tohono O'odham, Pueblo, Apache, and Navajo. Rumors of Zuni villages laden with precious jewels and metals called the Seven Golden Cities of Cibola drew the Spanish into the region.

The natives, at first friendly, offended by the constant demands for food and clothing and by the ill-treatment of their women, drove off the horses and mules of the Spaniards. The village involved was attacked [by the Spanish] and some of the men surrendered. The officer in charge prepared two hundred stakes for these prisoners but when the Indians saw they were to be roasted alive they seized the stakes and renewed the fight with the result that they all died more agreeable deaths.[47]

Later, Coronado was seriously injured in a fall from his horse, so the Spanish decided to go back to Mexico. Two monks remained behind to preach Christianity, but they were soon killed by the natives.

During the next fifty years, however, New Spain became a strong and powerful country. At least four Spanish expeditions into the area had traveled the length and breadth of Pueblo country, engaging the natives in battle and plundering their pueblos. In 1598, about four hundred armor-clad soldiers, colonists, and friars marched into the upper Rio Grande valley with eighty carts and one thousand head of cattle. The men were led by Juan de Oñate, and the purpose of his expedition was to Christianize the Pueblo people and to take over their lands for the country of Spain.

The Spanish arrived with ideas and cultural norms that were totally foreign to the

In 1540, Coronado, hoping to find the Seven Golden Cities of Cibola, sought out Zuni villages such as this one.

natives, and the two societies completely misunderstood each other. The Spaniards wanted strict allegiance to the Spanish king and the Christian faith. The natives simply wanted peace, and it is not clear that they understood the implications of the agreements they made with the invaders. An example of their polite but perhaps uncomprehending acceptance of Spanish terms is given by Edward H. Spicer in *Cycles of Conquest:*

> Wherever he went among the Rio Grande villages [Oñate] obtained agreements of "obedience" or submission. For example, at the Keres villages of Santo Domingo, Oñate met with seven caciques . . . who were said to represent thirty-four villages. A general meeting was held in which Oñate told them of the King of Spain, offered protection from their enemies, and described the meaning and importance of [Christian] baptism. At the conclusion, the seven caciques gave what the Spaniards understood as a pledge of allegiance to the king, and to Oñate as governor; then all knelt and kissed the hands of Oñate and Father Juan de Escalona who represented the Church. This ceremony was repeated elsewhere and thus, without bloodshed or overt resistance, Oñate began his program of colonization and missionization. There is no record of how the Indians interpreted the idea of obedi-

ence and submission, nor of their understanding of what Oñate proposed to carry out, but by the end of 1598 all the villages had made the pledge.[48]

The people of the Acoma Pueblo, however, were not ready to surrender their independence to the newcomers. They killed Oñate's personal aide, igniting a fight with seventy soldiers. The Spanish eventually captured five hundred Acoma people, who were sentenced to have one foot chopped off. Another battle ensued, and this time the Spaniards were forced to leave Acoma lands. A group of six hundred people from Acoma who were friendly to the Spanish settled below the mesa, while the others rebuilt their destroyed village. Hundreds had died in the battle.

Between 1610 and 1630, wave after wave of missionaries came into the area. In those twenty years, they constructed churches in all the pueblos, even in Taos in the far north. During the 1620s, secular and church officers such as governors and other civil officials were set up in all the villages. By 1630 there were Franciscan missionaries working out of twenty-five missions. Schools were established for teaching reading, writing, music, and trades to Native American children. And by that year the missionaries claimed to have baptized sixty thousand Pueblo people, although this figure has been called into question.

Father Benavidez, who described the various pueblos in 1630, claimed spectacular success in converting the residents:

[In] the Teoas (Taos) nation, with fifteen or sixteen pueblos, in which must be 7,000 souls, in a district of twelve or thirteen leagues [thirty-six to thirty-nine miles], all [are] baptized; with two monasteries, that is, the one of San Francisco de Sandia and that of San Antonio de la Isleta. At these are schools of reading and writing, singing, and playing of all instruments; and with much care in the polite . . . life. These two monasteries and churches are very beautiful and costly. . . . And all the other pueblos have also their beautiful churches.

Passing forward another four leagues, the Queres [Keres] nation commences with its first pueblo [that] of San Felipe, and extends more than ten leagues, in seven pueblos. There must be in them 4,000 souls, all baptized. There are three monasteries and churches, very costly and beautiful, aside from those which each pueblo has. These Indians are very dexterous in reading, writing, and playing on all instruments, and craftsmen in all the crafts [thanks to] the great Religious [monks] who converted them.[49]

Later writers, however, have suggested that the friars wrongly equated acceptance of baptism with sincerity of conversion, noting that the tribes have continued to practice their traditional religion even to this day. In the early seventeenth century, however, the villages were peaceful, and many among the new generations were accepting Spanish rule. In spite of this, great pain was inflicted upon the natives. The Salzmanns explain:

[T]he Pueblos were still being brutally dealt with by the Spanish colonists, the soldiers, and even the clergy. Conditions became so harsh that in 1655 the Hopi felt compelled to send a delegation to Santa Fe, the seat of the Spanish governor. Its mission was to denounce a priest for publicly whipping a Hopi and then setting him afire for "an act of idolatry."[50]

Not only were Pueblo people tortured and killed for practicing their religion, which the Europeans viewed as idolatrous, but the tribes were severely taxed by the Spanish, who demanded tribute in the form of food and goods to support their garrison at Santa Fe.

Revolt of 1680

By 1680 there were about twenty-four hundred Spanish ruling over thirty thousand Pueblo people in dozens of villages along the Rio Grande. Most of the Spanish were concentrated in Santa Fe, but some were living in Tewa country and other areas. A few had taken Pueblo wives or otherwise joined with the natives. Although the Spanish presence in the region was strong, the government had been in disarray for several decades, having installed fourteen Spanish governors in a space of fifty years. This administrative confusion was aggravated by severe droughts and crop failures from 1667 to 1672.

In contrast, several strong leaders had come into prominence among the pueblos. These men were helping revive the traditional religious practices of their tribes. One man with a great ability to organize, Popé, of San Juan Pueblo, was able to unite the pueblos in a common cause. According to Ickes: "Popé claimed supernatural authority for his pronouncements. He said that he held communication with the spirits of three Indians who had appeared to him in the kiva at Taos."[51]

By 1680, the uneasy coexistence between the Pueblo peoples and their Spanish rulers was about to end in violence. A revolt was planned, and to coordinate the tribes, Popé sent a knotted rope to each pueblo; every morning one knot was to be untied until the last was reached. On the day of the last knot, the tribes were to rise up and kill every friar and expel the Spanish from the region. Several friars learned of the conspiracy and sent word to the governor. Popé, in turn, learned of the leaks, and the attack was moved up a day. On August 10, the Great Rebellion of 1680 began. A force of men from the Tanos Pueblo besieged Santa Fe while Native Americans in the villages killed the missionaries and any other Spanish living there. When this was done, warriors from several more pueblos descended on Santa Fe, and Spanish resistance quickly collapsed. Spicer writes:

Within a few days all the missions had been destroyed, 21 out of 33 missionaries had been killed, and 375 of the 2,350 colonists had been wiped out. The fact that the majority of the Spaniards were allowed to escape indicated that the major objectives of the revolt were, first to eliminate the mission system and, second, to drive all the Spaniards out of Pueblo county. . . .

The unity displayed by the Rio Grande villages in carrying through the revolt was something new in the region. . . . It was an extreme reaction to an extreme situation. Spanish oppression and Spanish weakness had offered what seemed an unusual opportunity. . . . For the first time . . . in Pueblo history, a supra-village organization came into existence and focused . . . on a single objective of getting rid of the Spanish.[52]

After the Revolution

Freedom did not last long for the Pueblo tribes. Once the Spanish were driven from the area, the unity between the tribes quickly vanished. Several individuals made an attempt to turn Santa Fe into a Native American capital, but a lack of common purpose prevented such a grand scheme from succeeding. The Apache, instead of joining in a common cause with the victors against the Spanish, renewed raids on villages and farmlands, further weakening pueblo unity.

In 1692 the Spanish began a reconquest of the region. Some villages surrendered easily, others fought back but were hampered by the lack of a strong central leader and unified front. Spicer writes:

> The Keres villages of Zia, Santa Ana, and San Felipe submitted with no show of fight, while the other Keres villages of Cochiti and Santo Domingo resisted. Cochiti people fought vigorously and were quickly defeated, while the Santo Domingans left their village in ruins and joined the people of Jemez to the west for further resistance.

The Tanos split similarly. Those who had settled in Santa Fe . . . vowed obedience to [Spanish conqueror Diego]

A Pueblo chief watches over his village. While the Spanish suffered from poor leadership, the pueblo people had chiefs of great fortitude.

de Vargas in perfectly peaceful fashion. But the Tanos who had settled farther north among the Tewas did not submit and joined with San Ildefonso, the most resistant of the Tewa villages in continued defiance of de Vargas. The Black Mesa near San Ildefonso became a center for Indians who refused to accept de Vargas' domination. Here the Tanos, San Ildefonsans and other Tewas, and some from Cochiti, joined in a nine-months' resistance during 1694. From this headquarters they raided Santa Fe and harassed the Spaniards. Eventually all except some Tanos surrendered and again submitted to Spanish rule.[53]

By 1694, the Spanish were back in Santa Fe. After battling to retake the town, they executed seventy Native American resisters and sold four hundred women and children into slavery. Thus was the country retaken from its native inhabitants. Various uprisings, some more serious than others, were a constant occurrence, but the backbone of Native American rebellion had been broken in the region. Ickes writes:

> The conquest was finally complete, but a great number of Indians lost their lives and many pueblos were abandoned, never again to flourish as before, and New Mexico entered upon a period of Spanish rule which was to last for one hundred and twenty-two years (1700–1822).[54]

During this period, disease, famine, and raids by the Navajo and Apache drove down the population numbers of the Pueblo peoples. Of the thirty-five thousand or so natives who lived in the region at the beginning of the seventeenth century, only seventeen thousand were left alive by the beginning of the 1700s.

The Navajo in the New Era

The Navajo also took part in the revolt of 1680, and like the Pueblo peoples, were dealt with severely by the Spanish in the aftermath. But as a nomadic people, many Navajo were able to escape from the harsh treatment given to the sedentary Pueblo villages. In fact, many Pueblo leaders in the revolution fled their villages and took up with the Navajo to evade Spanish punishment. The result was a mixing of the spiritual and material cultures.

Historians believe that the Pueblo people brought a more structured cosmology and elaborate ritual performances to the Navajo, and Pueblo women carried with them advanced skills in weaving, pottery, and other arts. In addition, the symbolic importance of corn had increased by the early eighteenth century, and the plant was elevated to one of the central elements in the Navajo culture. Corn pollen was used in ceremonies to represent fertility and prosperity, and the fast, strong growth of the corn stalk was used to represent the Navajo people themselves.

The Navajo also benefited from the arrival of Spanish cattle, horses, and especially sheep. By the 1700s, the Navajo way of life revolved around the tribe's

The Navajo benefited greatly from the arrival of Spanish sheep. They used the wool to weave cloth and the meat provided protein.

sheep herds. Almost every man and woman had at least a few sheep, and children were given lambs to care for that would become part of their flocks in adulthood.

The wool of the sheep was used to weave cloth, and the meat provided a source of protein. With the use of horses the Navajo could graze the sheep over a wider area and drive them into the shade of the mountains during the hot summer season.

By adopting the best of the Pueblo and Spanish cultures, the Navajo were one of the few tribes in the region to expand and grow. Over time they embraced these cultural acquisitions and made them part of their legendary past. By the mid-nineteenth century, the Navajo had established a strong presence throughout the Four Corners region and were a force to be reckoned with when the territory became part of the United States.

The Apache in the Spanish Period

When the Spanish came to the southwest region, they rapidly replaced the Pueblo peoples as the Apache's principal trading partners. The cows and sheep the Spanish introduced to the region were valued by the Apache as a new food source. But it was the horse that most notably changed the Apache way of life. Within fifty years of Coronado's exploration into the region, the Apache had become experts at hunting, fighting, and raiding on horseback. The Jicarilla believed horses required great respect because they were a gift to the Apache from supernatural powers. They sang religious songs to honor the horse and treated their personal mounts with great kindness.

But as the years passed, the Spanish proved to be interested in the Apache only for use as slaves. Decades before the Great Rebellion of 1680, a constant state of warfare existed between the Europeans and the natives. Spanish horsemen attacked Apache camps, seizing captives, while the Apache constantly raided Spanish settlements, stealing horses, cattle, and guns.

The guerrilla tactics of the nomadic Apache were difficult for Spanish sol-

Most of the Apache raids on Spanish towns were conducted because the tribes needed basic necessities.

diers to repel. Between 1748 and 1770 the Apache conducted hundreds of successful raids on Spanish towns, killing at least four thousand settlers and destroying millions of dollars worth of property.

Although many raids were conducted for vengeance, the main reason for raiding was to supply the tribe with basic necessities. An unnamed Apache reveals this fact in *Apache Life-Way:*

When the people are poor and need supplies, the leader says, "We must go out and get what we need." It is volunteer work. Whoever is in want of food and necessities goes. The leader heads the party, which is made up of men only. Women never go on raids. . . .

If a man wouldn't go [on a raid], it was because he was generally lazy, just too lazy to get around, and his mind watery. . . . People who don't go [on raids] are just lazy people; that's all.[55]

Since the Spanish could not resist the expert tactics of the Apache raiders, they were forced to try a different approach. Beginning in 1786, the Spanish began to give the Apache people food, clothing, liquor, and guns in exchange for peace. The guns were inferior, but the alcohol weakened Apache society to such a point that the raiding ceased. This policy worked until 1821, when Mexico took over the region. The new rulers could not afford to buy peace, so the Apache raids started again.

Due to a weak governance based in faraway Spain, the Apache and other tribes in the region were often able to retain their lands, their cultures, and their spiritual beliefs largely intact. During some eras the Spanish were able to force their autocratic system on the tribes; at other times they were ineffectual. This precarious clash of cultures lasted until 1848, when the defenses the tribes had used to protect themselves from Spanish domination were put to the test by the unstoppable expansion of the United States.

Chapter 6

Living in the United States

By the early nineteenth century, the Spanish government had become so preoccupied with political events in Europe that they had virtually abandoned the attempt to subjugate the tribes in the Southwest. By 1812, only 121 Spanish soldiers remained in the region to defend a population of forty thousand Spanish settlers who were under constant attack from Apache raiders.

In addition, there were only twenty-two Spanish missionaries to oversee twenty-six pueblos. This reduction of clerical manpower resulted in a renewed flourishing of traditional religions among the Pueblo tribes. Yet the Spanish considered the Pueblo people to be "civilized" and relied on them as a link between their interests in the region and the "savage" Apache who were constantly disrupting trade and settlement.

The Mexican Era

In 1821, Mexico threw off the yoke of Spanish rule. With that declaration of independence, New Mexico and Arizona were no longer Spanish colonies, but part of the country of Mexico. This instituted a new era for Native Americans in the area. The Mexicans almost completely abandoned the Spanish mission system; by 1830, only five missionaries remained in the area. The tribes in the region became free to pursue their ceremonial life, which had been secretly sustained through centuries of persecution and oppression.

This isolation from the Mexican government also fostered a period of cooperation between the Pueblo villages and the rural Hispanic communities in the area. The two groups worked together on agricultural projects and commingled at tribal ceremonies and at feast days for Christian saints. The two cultures also joined defenses to unite against attacks by Navajo, Apache, and Ute raiders. This cultural exchange, however, was only seen in eastern settlements. Tribes such as the Zuni and Hopi continued to remain isolated and removed from Spanish and Mexican influence.

In Apache country, Native American raids had forced Mexican settlers to leave the area in droves. In his book *Commerce of the Prairies,* published in 1844, trader Josiah Gregg describes the situation:

> The depredations [attacks] of the Apaches have been of such long duration, that, beyond the immediate [outskirts] of the towns, the whole country from New Mexico to the borders of Durango [Colorado] is almost entirely depopulated. The haciendas and ranchos have been mostly abandoned, and the people chiefly confined to towns and cities.[56]

To stop the raids and killing, the Mexican government offered a bounty for the scalp of every Apache man, woman, and child murdered by Mexicans or Americans. This drew dozens of "scalp hunters" to the area who were willing to kill any Apache in order to collect one hundred dollars for the scalp of every man, fifty dollars for every woman, and twenty-five dollars for every child.

This policy resulted in the Apache becoming sworn enemies of Mexico. When Mexicans were captured by the Apache, they were turned over to the women for punishment. This treatment of Mexican prisoners by Chiricahua women was explained by an unnamed Apache in *An Apache Life-Way:*

> The Chiricahua treated Mexicans in a rough way when they were captured, but they didn't treat Americans like that. These Chiricahua were more the enemies of the Mexicans than of any other people on earth, because the Mexicans treated these Chiricahua in a nasty way.

Pueblo people work outside their terraced houses. The departure of Spanish missionaries allowed traditional Pueblo religion to flourish.

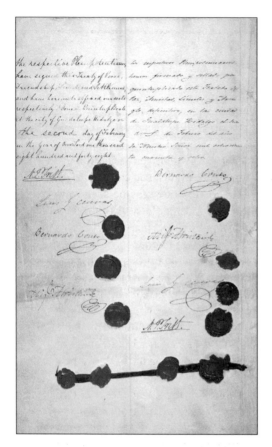

The Treaty of Guadalupe Hidalgo, signed on February 2, 1848, ended the Mexican era.

They say they used to tie Mexicans with their hands behind their backs. Then they turned the women loose with axes and knives to kill the Mexican prisoner. The man could hardly run, and the women would chase him around until they killed him. . . .

When a brave warrior is killed, the men go out for about three Mexicans. They bring them back for the women to kill in revenge. The women ride at them on horseback, armed with spears.[57]

The Arrival of the Americans

The Mexican era ended on February 2, 1848, when the United States and Mexico signed the Treaty of Guadalupe Hidalgo after several years of war. The treaty ceded 1.2 million square miles of Mexican territory to the United States, including most of New Mexico, Arizona, Colorado, Utah, Nevada, and California. The Mexicans received $15 million and other considerations. The two sides, however, paid little thought to the Native Americans who had lived on the land before either nation had even existed.

The treaty brought rapid changes to Native Americans in the Southwest. American settlers flooded into the region and the U.S. government quickly sent American soldiers into the area to exert control over the new territories. The Americans wanted to isolate the Native American tribes on reservations and exploit the lands for their wealth of minerals, lumber, water, and other natural resources.

The Americans dismissed any claims the natives had on the land. The opposing attitudes concerning land rights were summed up in the book *The Southwestern Frontier—1865–1881*. Historian Carl Coke Rister, writing in 1928, uses derogatory stereotypes that were typical at that time:

Since a large portion of this vast region abounded in animal and veg-

An American's View of Santa Fe

In 1865, as a consequence of continued battles with Native Americans in the West, the U.S. Congress ordered an inquiry into the "present condition of the Indian tribes." A special committee was formed to travel to Colorado, New Mexico, and elsewhere. A member of the committee, Dr. Samuel B. Davis, recorded his thoughts in a journal. One entry was about the condition of poor people in Santa Fe, most of whom were Native Americans, · Mexicans, and those of mixed raced. It was reprinted in *Chronicle of a Congressional Journey,* edited by Lonnie J. White. Davis wrote:

"Santa Fe has a population of about 12,000. How they subsist is a mystery to all who travel through the country. There is, indeed, much suffering among the poor and middle classes, many of whom die, if not of starvation, for want of wholesome food. Most of the houses are very much crowded, and in addition to the men, women and children, in almost every one may be seen from one to a dozen domestic animals— dogs, goats, sheep and burros. This latter little animal . . . is the main support of many a poor family. [Burros] are used to transport wood, water and merchandise. It is not unusual to see droves of from six to twenty coming down from the mountains, each with a bundle of wood strapped on his back. Wood is sold for so much a burro load— about seventy-five cents. . . . Red pepper, onions and goats-milk comprise all the food of [the] poor, their principal occupation, sleeping and

In 1865 the United States discovered that the population of Santa Fe was suffering from starvation and dire poverty.

etable life, the nomadic tribes occupying it were determined not to allow encroachments by the rising tide of immigration of white people directed that way. The struggle between the native races and the newcomers . . . carried on with an increasing degree of intensity as the savages were pushed on and on toward the west. Realizing that this was the last portion of unsettled regions of the Southwest the hostile savages were ready to assert their traditional rights to this domain, and the frontiersmen were equally determined to drive them out and occupy it. This attitude on the part of these two races resulted in one of the most [bloody] struggles ever carried out on our American frontier. "Moonlight raids," and even day-light depredations, were frequently made on the frontier by the wild Indians, while punitive expeditions and organized campaigns by way of reprisals were conducted by the settlers.[58]

Rister went on to justify the "stern struggle" by noting that the area at stake offered great promise for the development of a profitable cattle industry and a productive agricultural center.

Eventually the Apache were pushed onto reservations where inadequate game and lack of other resources left the tribes on the brink of starvation. According to the website maintained by the San Carlos Apache Tribe Cultural Center:

As part of life on the reservation we became dependent on the handouts issued to us by the government of the United States. Often the rations failed to meet our basic needs, during the early reservation years food and supplies promised by the government were often sold off by dishonest Indian Agents [federal workers], leaving us with shortages of food, cloth, or wood for cooking and warming our homes. In desperation our people left the reservation to hunt, gather plants and raid in traditional ways. These forays to relieve our poverty were commonly referred to as "outbreaks" in the local press. We were branded criminals in the struggle to maintain our dignity.[59]

Clash of Religions

Nowhere was the clash of cultures between white America and Native Americans more obvious than on the issue of religion. Tom Bahti gives some highlights of this prolonged battle:

In the 1870s and '80s the U.S. government adopted a policy of turning over the task of educating and "civilizing" Indians to the churches, and various Christian denominations were assigned to specific reservations. The practice was discontinued in the 1890s but not before the influence of some twenty-seven Christian sects became established among a number of tribes, particularly those whose native culture was in a state of disintegration.

About this same time the Bureau of Indian Affairs made a number of attempts to suppress native religion with a series of departmental regulations. . . . This anti-Indian movement culminated in 1889 with a set of regulations known as the Code of Religious Offenses. It was used as late as the 1920s in an attempt to crush Pueblo religion, restricting the times of the year and days of the week for native religious observances. It even restricted the number of participants and set age limits—all in an attempt to deny younger Indians the opportunity to participate and learn.[60]

Finally, in 1934, this decades-old policy was discontinued. John Collier, the new Commissioner of Indian Affairs, issued a directive that said: "No interference with Indian religious life or ceremonial expression will hereafter be tolerated. The cultural liberty of Indians is in all respects to be considered equal to that of any non-Indian group."[61]

Christianity did have a lasting impact on southwestern Native American religions. A minority of people completely abandoned their native religion to accept what the Navajo call "the Jesus Way." A majority of people simply modified the religion introduced by the Spaniards to fit with their native practices, using the framework provided by Christianity without discarding the old beliefs. Others combined native and Christian beliefs to form an entirely new religious movement called the Native American Church. Tribes such as the Hopi and Zuni continue to practice the ancient religions with a near total exclusion of Christian beliefs.

A minority of Native Americans abandoned their native religion and became Christians. Here, a young Native American wears Christian crosses.

Pueblos in the Twentieth Century

The world of white America began to close in on the Pueblos in 1881 when the transcontinental railroad came to Gallup, New Mexico, eventually bringing tens of thousands of settlers into the region. Along with the settlers came a wave of tourists who invaded the pueblos with cameras. This was a mixed blessing, but the loss of privacy was tolerated when the outsiders began to pay good prices for Pueblo pottery, jewelry, paintings, and other crafts. In addition to the cash, however, the influx of visitors brought with them tuberculosis and other diseases which continued to take their toll on the Pueblo populations. And despite the profits generated by native crafts, the issue of land ownership remained the central problem for the Puebloan peoples.

There had been little land available for cultivation before the arrival of the white settlers, and by 1912 San Juan Pueblo had lost 75 percent of its farmable lands and San Ildefonso 80 percent. And about twelve thousand non-Native American settlers were living on Pueblo land. As a result, the Puebloan peoples could no

The tourists who followed white settlers to New Mexico began to purchase jewelry and other Pueblo crafts.

The Tourist and Art Trade

In 1881, the Atchison, Topeka, and Santa Fe Railroad was completed from Kansas City to Santa Fe. As a result, vacationing tourists from other regions of the United States began to visit the Southwest in large numbers.

By 1925 the Santa Fe Railroad was running carefully organized "Indian Detours" onto Native American lands in specially designed motor coaches that featured swivel seats so tourists could get a complete view of the countryside. Passengers were encouraged to take the three-day sidetrips that were led by female guides called "Couriers," who held comprehensive knowledge of Native American arts, crafts, and rituals. As the trips grew more popular, even isolated Hopi and Navajo lands became stopping places for tour buses. As the years passed, the improvement of roads made tourist automobile trips in the area commonplace.

With the tourist trade came a revival of Native American art. Native American artists recognized that the sale of arts and crafts was a new, desirable source of income on the cash-poor reservations—and a way to preserve their independence.

Today hundreds of Native American artists thrive in the region, and the art galleries of Santa Fe, Taos, and elsewhere have provided a way for American society to understand native attitudes. As artist J. J. Brody observed in *When the Rainbow Touches Down:* "[T]he craft revivals established a new relationships between Indians and a small but influential and articulate element of White society, making it possible for Indians . . . to have more dignity and independence than at any time before."

longer rely on their traditional agriculture and turned to tourism and day labor to survive.

As America moves into the twenty-first century, however, the fifty-five thousand people who make up the tribes of the pueblos are still strong and continue to live on their ancestral lands, keeping their ancient traditions alive. According to the Indian Pueblo Cultural Center website:

Today, after suffering disruption by gold-seeking Europeans, alien Indian tribes and Anglo-American westward expansion, the Pueblo people are settled in nineteen communities, some of which have been continuously inhabited since long before the discovery of America. Still retaining their ancient and largely secret ceremonial life, they nevertheless welcome visitors from all over the world, and offer a glimpse of the proud heritage which they have kept alive for more than a thousand years.[62]

The Survival of the Navajo

Although the Navajo were able to coexist with the Spanish, the American era is one of the most tragic in their long history. Mary Roberts Coolidge writes that the Navajo "were hated by the Mexicans and Pueblos, and, isolated and wandering as they had been, they knew scarcely anything of the alien white people who were to be their rulers."[63]

The Navajo clashed periodically with the Americans almost as soon as the United States took possession of the southwest ter-

ritories. Then in April 1863, after wiping out the Mescalero Apache, Brigadier General James H. Carleton, representing the U.S. government, ordered the Navajo to move to a forty-acre reservation outside of a circular grove of cottonwoods known as the Bosque Redondo at Fort Sumter. The Navajo refused to surrender their freedom.

Carleton issued an order stating that any Navajo who did not surrender by July 20, 1863, would be considered "hostile" and military actions would be taken. He also ordered a regiment of one thousand soldiers to present-day Gallup to enforce his order.

July 20 came and went but the Native Americans did not surrender. Carleton moved against the tribes in a six-month

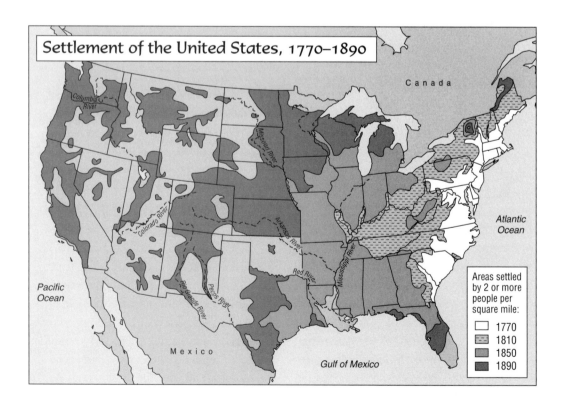

Settlement of the United States, 1770–1890

Canada

Columbia River

Missouri River

Colorado River

Arkansas River

Red River

Mississippi River

Rio Grande River

Pecos River

Pacific Ocean

Atlantic Ocean

Mexico

Gulf of Mexico

Areas settled by 2 or more people per square mile:
☐ 1770
▨ 1810
▨ 1850
■ 1890

campaign during which he sought to destroy Navajo independence. U.S. soldiers seized huge herds of Navajo sheep, destroyed their crops across a wide area, cut down their ancient fruit trees, and burnt their dwellings. Faced with the prospect of massive starvation at the end of 1864, nearly eight thousand Navajo surrendered. They were forced to march over three hundred miles to Bosque Redondo on what became known as the "Long Walk."

Once interred at the fort, survival was impossible for many. The water supply was tainted, promised food rations never arrived, and crops were destroyed by drought. By 1865, the Navajo were begging Carleton to let them leave but the general refused to admit his policy had failed. The federal government's Indian superintendent personally observed the squalid conditions that were forced upon the Native Americans, and in 1868 the Navajo were freed under the terms of a new treaty. A ten-mile long column of Navajo followed by huge herds of sheep wound their way back to the lands of their ancestors. In the meantime, thousands of men, women, and children had died because of Carleton's failed policy.

A 3.5-million acre reservation was set up for the surviving Navajo in the Four Corners region under the terms of the treaty. Over the years, that reservation has been expanded several times and today it encompasses 15 million acres—an area larger than the state of Massachusetts. As of 1999, more than 250,000 Navajo live on and off the reservation.

Navajo-Hopi Land Dispute

Before their lives were interrupted by the U.S. government, the Navajo led fairly prosperous lives in the Four Corners region. Their flocks of sheep grew ever larger as their population swelled. By 1819 the Navajo were living and grazing their herds within two miles of the Hopi village on First Mesa. This interfered with the Hopi way of life since the land provided firewood as well as area for grazing their herds and the planting of crops. When the U.S. Army forced the Navajo to Bosque Redondo the Hopi reclaimed these lands.

After the Navajo returned to the area conflicts between the tribes began again. In 1882, the U.S. government set aside an area of about fifty-five miles by seventy miles for exclusive use by the Hopi. The secretary of the Interior Department, however, was allowed to decide if other tribes could settle there at a later date, and where they could live on the reservation. The Hopi population remained stable but the Navajo population continued to grow. As the years passed the government permitted the Navajo to occupy more and more of the Hopi lands. Exasperated, the Hopi filed suit in an Arizona court in 1958 to remove the Navajo from lands they believed to be theirs.

The lawsuit wound its way through the courts until 1962, when Arizona gave the Hopi sole use of one part of the reservation and ordered the Hopi and Navajo to share the remaining 1.8 million acres. This shared land became known as the Joint Use Area (JUA). This division did little to stop the land-use issues which continued

Mining Uranium for Atomic Bombs

When the United States government began to build atomic bombs in the 1940s and 1950s, they needed a steady supply of highly toxic uranium ore to fuel the weapons of mass destruction. The major supply was found in the Four Corners area of the Southwest, the heart of Navajo country. Peter H. Eichstaedt writes about the dangers to Navajo miners who dug the substance from the earth in *If You Poison Us:*

"About a quarter of the miners were Native Americans, mostly Navajos, who labored in the uranium mines and processing mills. They dug the uranium ore with pick and shovel in the small mines called 'dog holes' . . . breathing [poisonous] radon gas and silica-laden dust. They ate food tainted with uranium oxide and drank the contaminated water that dripped from the mine walls. They carried uranium home to their wives and children on their shoes, clothes, and bodies. Yet, in the face of mounting evidence and warnings from Public Health Service physicians, mining companies and government agencies refused to acknowledge that there was danger—that the miners were harvesting their own death. . . .

Today Native Americans continue to reap a bitter harvest for their patriotic role in World War II and the Cold War. Undetermined tons of exposed radioactive mine waste remain on native lands. Rainwater has leached uranium byproducts and toxic metals into underground water, with potentially long-lasting consequences. Small uranium pit mines remain open, filled with water, inviting children to swim and animals to drink. At Laguna Pueblo, an open-pit mine that covers nearly 3,000 acres remained untouched for seven years after operations stopped, until the pueblo itself started reclamation."

A man displays two Pueblo pots that were made from uranium mine clay.

to create hostilities between the two tribes for more than a decade. Congress was forced to intervene in 1974, dividing the land arbitrarily between the two tribes. As a result 2,650 Navajo families living in the Hopi area were ordered to leave, and 24 Hopi families were ordered to evacuate the Navajo area. Uprooting these families, some who had lived in these areas for generations, caused new problems and bitter feelings erupted.

As the January 1, 2000, deadline for Navajo relocation approached, about 125 Navajo families had not moved and tension was mounting. The difficulty of this long-running dispute is summed up by the Salzmanns:

> On the one hand, the Navajo Reservation population, more than twenty times larger than the Hopi population, has been growing rapidly, and families that have sizable herds of sheep in an arid or semiarid environment need large areas for grazing. On the other hand, the Hopi are eager to hold on to what they consider their ancient homeland and to protect their fields from sheep, who in a few hours can destroy the results of long and careful cultivation.[64]

The Pima and Tohono O'odham in the United States

Between 1874 and 1917, the United States government established six Pima reservations. Those who lived along the Gila River found that their water supply was diverted by white farmers upstream. Without water, the Native American crops withered and died in the scorching sun. Pima farmers were forced to work in the fields of white farmers for low wages. Little farming is done on the Gila River Reservation today.

In 1929, Mary Roberts Coolidge wrote about the continuing struggles of the Pima as white settlers were flooding into the southern Arizona region:

> The history of the Pimas for the last thirty years is told in the struggle for their ancient rights to water in the Gila River. From time immemorial they had supported themselves by agriculture. After the Apaches ceased to harry them, they were prosperous and progressive, until about 1900, when their water supply began to be cut off by settlers above the reservation. As early as 1899, engineers of the United States Geological Survey called attention to their perilous situation. . . .

> But from this time on the supply decreased. [A government Indian agent wrote:] "Year after year they plowed and sowed and irrigated their crops only to have them destroyed by drought before maturity." The Indians began to eke out a scanty living by hauling wood and other precarious work, and some became dependent on charity.[65]

The situation was not much different for the Tohono O'odham in their homeland, referred to as Papagueria by Coolidge:

Cut off from their water supply by white farmers, Pima tribes suffered the withering of their crops—including corn.

From 1885 onward, [the Tohono O'odham] began to suffer from white encroachments. Mining companies moved into Papagueria and used up the mesquite wood, depriving the Indians of the annual crop of beans; cattle companies began to graze their stock on Tohono O'odham lands and usurped the scanty water. . . .

[Without water to grow crops] the men take outside work on ranches, railroads, in the mines, and are regarded as excellent workers. . . . At the other end of the social scale there are perhaps about a thousand wandering Papagos along the border who live mostly on desert products.[66]

A New Generation

Many older Native Americans alive today in the Southwest lived through a time when the males were forced to cut their hair and attend "Indian schools" to learn the ways of white people. If they spoke one word of their native language, their teachers washed their mouths out with soap. They live today on reservations, some in homes with no electricity or running water.

Although their grandchildren often live in town, play basketball, and watch television, the elders are teaching the members of the young generation to weave, cook, and herd sheep just as their ancestors have done. As the sixty-four-year-old Navajo Edward Begay said in an interview with Lyric Wallwork Winik in *Parade* magazine: "You want to make your children like a double-edged axe. Sharp on both ends, English and Navajo. If you only learn one side, like the white man's way, you'll be lost on the other side. You want them to be sharp at both ends."[67]

It is difficult for young Native Americans today to maintain that balance. According to Winik, the average income for people on the southwest reservations is less than half that of white Americans. About 31 percent live below the poverty line, as opposed to 13 percent for the U.S. population as a whole. Suicide rates are 70 percent higher on reservations than elsewhere, and only 41 percent of Navajo people on the reservation are high school graduates.

Although these statistics are troubling, on another level, the tribes made great strides in the twentieth century. Population numbers continue to increase and Native Americans are the nation's youngest and fastest-growing minority,

Students pose for a photo at an "Indian school," where many white teachers attempted to anglicize their Native American students.

with 40 percent of tribe members under the age of twenty. Casinos, such as the ones run by the Pima-Maricopa in Arizona, are bringing large amounts of money to the reservations for the first time ever.

Tribes are applying casino profits to education, economic development, tribal courts, and infrastructure improvement such as building new houses, new schools, new roads, and new sewer and water systems. This money also benefits individuals by funding social service programs, scholarships, health care clinics, chemical dependency treatment programs, and other uses. But casinos have benefited only a small number of tribes. The rest are still struggling to lift themselves out of a centuries-old cycle of poverty and abuse by the federal government.

As the world enters the twenty-first century, many Native Americans feel that they have much to teach the rest of humanity about culture, art, spirituality, and the natural world—not as a subject of study in a book, but as modern, contributing members of society. As a Native American named Mad Bear succinctly points out:

If there is anyone on this Earth who can speak for our people, who can talk of our history and our ways, who can tell of our ancestors, who can say our future, it is the American Indian. We can speak for ourselves. . . . Our people have been widely researched but seldom consulted. We've been more a subject for study than a source for knowledge. And now we've been relegated to the past. Well, we live here in the present just like everyone else. And I mean here—right here— not in your textbooks or your libraries or your movies. We are here, and you are living our lives in the midst of our tribal lands and traditions. You will come to know us as we make ourselves known to you.[68]

Notes

Introduction: Under the Turquoise Sky

1. Quoted in Mary Roberts Coolidge, *The Rain-Makers*. 1929. Reprint, Santa Fe, NM: William Gannon, 1975, p. 2.
2. Zdenek Salzmann and Joy M. Salzmann, *Native Americans of the Southwest*. Boulder, CO: Westview Press, 1997, p. 2.

Chapter 1: Tribes of the Southwest

3. Coolidge, *The Rain-Makers,* pp. 7–8.
4. Will H. Robinson, *Under Turquoise Skies*. New York: Macmillan, 1928, p. 252.
5. Coolidge, *The Rain-Makers,* p. 3.
6. Larry DiLucchio, ed., Navajo Central Website, "Facts About Life on the Navajo Nation," April 29, 1999. http://navajocentral.org/faq02a.htm.
7. Edgar L. Hewett, *Ancient Life in the American Southwest*. Indianapolis: Bobbs-Merrill, 1930, p. 45.
8. Pueblo Cultural Center, "Indian Pueblo Cultural Center," July 13, 1999. www.indianpueblo.org/.
9. Hopi Information Network, "Hopi Homework FAQ," May 1998. www.info magic.com/~abyte/hopi/homework/faq.htm.

Chapter 2: Pueblos, Clans and Family Life

10. Quoted in Anna Wilmarth Ickes, *Mesa Land: The History and Romance of the American Southwest*. Boston: Houghton Mifflin, 1933, p. 123.
11. Ickes, *Mesa Land,* p. 125.
12. Matilda Coxe Stevenson, *Zuni Indians*. Glorieta, NM: Rio Grande Press, 1970, p. 349.
13. Pliny Earle Goddard, *Indians of the Southwest*. New York: American Museum Press, 1921, p. 72.
14. Leslie Spier, *Yuman Tribes of the Gila River*. 1933. Reprint, New York: Cooper Square Publishers, 1970, p 82.
15. Goddard, *Indians of the Southwest,* p. 92.
16. Stevenson, *Zuni Indians,* p. 291.
17. DiLucchio, "Facts About Life on the Navajo Nation."
18. Coolidge, *The Rain-Makers,* p. 55.
19. Quoted in Morris Edward Opler, *An Apache Life-Way*. New York: Cooper Square Publishers, 1965, pp. 153–54.
20. S. M. Barrett, ed., *Geronimo's Story of His Life*. New York: Duffield, 1906, p. 38.
21. Goddard, *Indians of the Southwest,* p. 96.

Chapter 3: Seasons of Survival

22. Goddard, *Indians of the Southwest*, p. 79.

23. Quoted in Goddard, *Indians of the Southwest*, p. 80.

24. Coolidge, *The Rain-Makers*, p. 50.

25. Carl Lumholtz, *New Trails in Mexico*. Glorieta, NM: Rio Grande Press, 1971, pp. 330–31.

26. S. M. Barrett, *Geronimo: His Own Story*. New York: E. P. Dutton, 1970, pp. 77–78.

27. Salzmann and Salzmann, *Native Americans of the Southwest*, p. 70.

28. Salzmann and Salzmann, *Native Americans of the Southwest*, p. 81.

29. Stevenson, *Zuni Indians*, p. 374 .

30. Stevenson, *Zuni Indians*, p. 374 .

31. Salzmann and Salzmann, *Native Americans of the Southwest*, p. 85.

32. Edna Mae Bennett, *Turquoise and the Indian*. Chicago: Swallow Press, 1966, p. 8.

33. Quoted in Bennett, *Turquoise and the Indian*, p. 22.

34. Quoted in Bennett, *Turquoise and the Indian*, p. 41.

Chapter 4: Spirits and Healing

35. Tom Bahti, *Southwestern Indian Ceremonials*. Las Vegas, NV: KC Publications, 1992, p. 26.

36. Goddard, *Indians of the Southwest*, p. 101.

37. Quoted in Edgar L. Hewett and Bertha P. Dutton, *The Pueblo Indian World*. Albuquerque: University of New Mexico Press, 1945, p. 136.

38. Hewett and Dutton, *The Pueblo Indian World*, p. 42.

39. Barrett, *Geronimo: His Own Story*, pp. 76–77.

40. Ron McCoy, *Archaeoastronomy*. Flagstaff, Museum of Northern Arizona, 1992, p. 3.

41. McCoy, *Archaeoastronomy*, p. 9.

42. Goddard, *Indians of the Southwest*, p. 135.

43. Quoted in Opler, *An Apache Life-Way*, p. 192.

44. Stevenson, *Zuni Indians*, p. 384.

Chapter 5: Clash of Cultures

45. Bernal Díaz del Castillo, *The Conquest of New Spain*. New York: Penguin Books, 1963, p. 216.

46. Quoted in Salzmann and Salzmann, *Native Americans of the Southwest*, p. 30.

47. Goddard, *Indians of the Southwest*, p. 60.

48. Edward H. Spicer, *Cycles of Conquest*. Tucson: University of Arizona Press, 1970, p. 156.

49. Quoted in Hewett and Dutton, *The Pueblo Indian World*, p. 133.

50. Salzmann and Salzmann, *Native Americans of the Southwest*, p. 25.

51. Ickes, *Mesa Land*, p. 34.

52. Spicer, *Cycles of Conquest*, p. 163.

53. Spicer, *Cycles of Conquest*, p. 164.

54. Ickes, *Mesa Land*, p. 40.

55. Quoted in Opler, *An Apache Life-Way,* p. 333.

Chapter 6: Living in the United States

56. Josiah Gregg, *Commerce of the Prairies.* Ann Arbor, MI: University Microfilms, 1966, p. 293.

57. Quoted in Opler, *An Apache Life-Way,* p. 351.

58. Carl Coke Rister, *The Southwestern Frontier—1865–1881: A History of the Coming of the Settlers, Indian Depredations and Massacres, Ranching Activities, Operations of White Desperadoes and Thieves, Government Protection, Building of Railways, and the Disappearance of the Frontier.* Cleveland: Arthur H. Clark, 1928, pp. 29–30.

59. San Carlos Apache Tribe Cultural Center, www.carizona.com/super/attractions/ san_carlos.html.

60. Bahti, *Southwestern Indian Ceremonials,* p. 4.

61. Bahti, *Southwestern Indian Ceremonials,* p. 4.

62. Pueblo Cultural Center, "Indian Pueblo Cultural Center," September 1, 1999. www.indianpueblo.org.

63. Coolidge, *The Rain-Makers,* p. 251.

64. Salzmann and Salzmann, *Native Americans of the Southwest,* p. 49.

65. Coolidge, *The Rain-Makers,* pp. 294–95.

66. Coolidge, *The Rain-Makers,* pp. 298–99.

67. Quoted in Lyric Wallwork Winik, "We Are Our Destiny," *Parade,* July 18, 1999, p. 6.

68. Quoted in Tryntje Van Ness Seymour, *When the Rainbow Touches Down.* Phoenix, AZ: The Heard Museum, 1988, p. 1.

For Further Reading

Tom Bahti, *Southwestern Indian Ceremonials*. Las Vegas, NV: KC Publications, 1992. A book that explores the spirituality, dances, and ceremonies of southwestern tribes in a big, colorful format full of beautiful drawings, mythical symbols, and kaleidoscopic paintings. Written by an advocate of Native American autonomy who was also an authority on Native American art and a graduate of the Anthropology Department of the University of New Mexico.

S. M. Barrett, ed., *Geronimo's Story of His Life*. New York: Duffield, 1906. This is the story of Geronimo's life as told by the Apache chief himself. A touching and poetic look at Apache life in the American Southwest in the nineteenth century.

Nancy Bonvillain, *The Hopi*. New York: Chelsea House, 1994. A book from the Indians of North America series that focuses on the life ways, history, and culture of the Hopi people.

———, *The Zuni*. New York: Chelsea House, 1995. Another book from the Indians of North America series, this one concerning the rich culture of the Zuni people.

Henry F. Dobyns, *The Pima-Maricopa*. New York: Chelsea House, 1989. Written by an anthropologist who has taught at Cornell, this book covers the lives and histories of the Native Americans who live in Arizona.

Thomas H. Flaherty, *Mound Builders and Cliff Dwellers*. Alexandria, VA: Time-Life Books, 1992. Half of this book covers the ancient Native American tribes who built huge mounds in Ohio and the Midwest. The second half concerns the cliff-dwelling Ancestral Pueblo people in Canyon de Chelly and other sites in the Southwest.

Peter Iverson, *The Navajo*. New York: Chelsea House, 1990. A detailed book about the Navajo people, their history, their religious practices, and their culture today.

Ron McCoy, *Archaeoastronomy*. Flagstaff: Museum of Northern Arizona, 1992. Archaeoastronomers are people who specialize in the study of ancient astronomical practices. This short book is published by the Museum of Northern Arizona and contains gorgeous pictures of southwestern stars, moonrises, and sunsets along with cosmic rock carvings, sand paintings, and other tribal representations of the universe.

Michael E. Melody, *The Apache.* New York: Chelsea House, 1989. This book covers the many and varied lifeways of the nomadic Apache bands including the Jicarilla, Lipan, Mescalero, Chiricahua, and Western Apache.

Edmund Nequatewa, *Truth of a Hopi.* 1936. Reprint, Flagstaff: Museum of Northern Arizona, 1967. First printed in 1936 by a Hopi author, this book contains page after page of stories relating to the origin, myths, and clan histories of the Hopi people.

Morris Edward Opler, *An Apache Life-Way.* 1941. Reprint, New York: Cooper Square Publishers, 1965. This book has hundreds of quotes from elder Chiricahua Apaches pertaining to ancient customs involving childhood, marriage, social relations, spiritual beliefs, and more.

Tryntje Van Ness Seymour, *When the Rainbow Touches Down.* Phoenix, AZ: The Heard Museum, 1988. This book features artists, artwork, and the stories behind Apache, Navajo, Rio Grande Pueblo, and Hopi paintings on display in the Heard Museum in Phoenix. Page after page of artwork is interspersed with thoughts by the artists themselves.

Teresa VanEtten, *Ways of Indian Wisdom.* Santa Fe, NM: Sunstone Press, 1987. VanEtten grew up at the San Juan Pueblo, where her family owned a trading post. This work is a collection of Pueblo legends composed of twenty stories translated from Tewa.

Henry Woodhead, ed., *People of the Desert.* Alexandria, VA: Time-Life Books, 1993. Another book in the informative The American Indians series, this one covering the past and present lives of the Pueblo, Navajo, Apache, Pima, Tohono O'odham, and other southwestern tribes. Dozens of beautiful color photos and drawings bring southwestern Native American history to life.

Works Consulted

Books

Edna Mae Bennett, *Turquoise and the Indian*. Chicago: Swallow Press, 1966. This book is all about turquoise, the stone that holds so much value for southwestern tribes. The author details ancient native mining and jewelry techniques, use of the stone in religious ceremonies, and a wide array of other turquoise information. The book includes many source quotes from Spanish explorers and more recent scientists and archaeologists.

Mary Roberts Coolidge, *The Rain-Makers*. Santa Fe, NM: William Gannon, 1975. This book provides a sympathetic look at the Native American tribes in the Southwest with chapters concerning social life, arts and industries, ceremonies and song, mythology, and other cultural aspects.

Byron Cummings, *First Inhabitants of Arizona and the Southwest*. Tucson, AZ: Cummings Publication Council, 1953. A book about the life and history of the ancient tribes who inhabited Arizona and the Southwest in ancient times. Filled with hundreds of pictures, diagrams, and drawings, including pottery designs and pueblo photos.

Bernal Díaz del Castillo, *The Conquest of New Spain*. New York: Penguin Books, 1963. A fascinating eyewitness account from the sixteenth century that details the first Spanish encounters with the Aztecs in Mexico.

Peter H. Eichstaedt, *If You Poison Us*. Santa Fe, NM: Red Crane Books, 1994. This book is about Navajo miners in the Four Corners region who were exposed to highly poisonous uranium between 1950 and 1980 as they dug for the radioactive materials used to build nuclear bombs. The book details the devastating physical, psychological, and cultural impact on the Navajo people and their lands.

Pliny Earle Goddard, *Indians of the Southwest*. New York: American Museum Press, 1921. Goddard was the Curator of Ethnology at the American Museum of Natural History in New York and was considered an early twentieth-century expert on the Pueblo, Navajo, Apache, Tohono O'odham, and other tribes in the region.

Josiah Gregg, *Commerce of the Prairies.* 1844. Reprint, Ann Arbor, MI: University Microfilms, 1966. This book by "Indian trader" Gregg was first published in 1844 and is widely recognized as the first description of the Southwest by a white American during the period of Santa Fe trade between Mexico and the United States.

Edgar L. Hewett, *Ancient Life in the American Southwest.* Indianapolis: Bobbs-Merrill, 1930. The author, who was the director of the School of American Research of the Archaeological Institute of America, was an expert on the ancient tribes that once inhabited Arizona, New Mexico, and other southwest regions.

Edgar L. Hewett and Bertha P. Dutton, *The Pueblo Indian World.* Albuquerque: University of New Mexico Press, 1945. A book about the Pueblo tribal civilization, languages, history, and spiritual practices.

Anna Wilmarth Ickes, *Mesa Land: The History and Romance of the American Southwest.* Boston: Houghton Mifflin, 1933. This book contains thorough coverage of southwestern tribes.

Carl Lumholtz, *New Trails in Mexico.* 1912. Reprint, Glorieta, NM: Rio Grande Press, 1971. Half travel guide, half anthropological study, this book is about the author's one-year exploration in the Sonoran desert in Arizona and Mexico.

Carl Coke Rister, *The Southwestern Frontier—1865–1881: A History of the Coming of the Settlers, Indian Depredations and Massacres, Ranching Activities, Operations of White Desperadoes and Thieves, Government Protection, Building of Railways, and the Disappearance of the Frontier.* Cleveland: Arthur H. Clark, 1928. The long subtitle of this book describes its content. The author's cultural biases, not unusual for this time, are candidly expressed.

Will H. Robinson, *Under Turquoise Skies.* New York: Macmillan, 1928. One of many travel guides from this era that was designed to entice easterners to explore the southwest region. Contains useful information about the tribes in the area.

Zdenek Salzmann and Joy M. Salzmann, *Native Americans of the Southwest.* Boulder, CO: Westview Press, 1997. This is a modern and concise guide to native tribes in the southwest region written by a professor emeritus of anthropology from the University of Massachusetts in collaboration with his wife. The book details ancient and contemporary peoples of the region, describing their life, art, and cultural achievements.

Edward H. Spicer, *Cycles of Conquest.* Tucson: University of Arizona Press, 1970. Spicer is a professor of anthropology at the University of Arizona who had first-hand acquaintanceships with southwestern Native Americans beginning in the 1930s. This book describes in vivid detail the Native American tribes as they suffered under the steady march of conquest by the Spanish, Mexicans, and Americans in the Southwest.

Leslie Spier, *Yuman Tribes of the Gila River.* 1933. Reprint, New York: Cooper Square Publishers, 1970. This book describes the lifestyles and cultures of Native American tribes in Arizona.

Matilda Coxe Stevenson, *Zuni Indians.* 1904. Reprint, Glorieta, NM: Rio Grande Press, 1970. This book is a reprint of the twenty-third Annual Report of the Bureau of American Ethnology of the Smithsonian Institution. The book is meticulously researched and contains more than 220 color and black-and-white photos, paintings, and drawings of the Zuni tribal lifestyle from the turn of the twentieth century. Long sections contain vivid details of Zuni gods, ceremonies, and religious practices.

H. Henrietta Stockel, *Survival of the Spirit: Chiricahua Apaches in Captivity.* Reno: University of Nevada Press, 1993. The Chiricahua Apaches, who had fought the U.S. government in an attempt to retain their ancestral hunting grounds, were captured and held in damp, humid prison camps. This book describes their destruction from diseases incurred in federal facilities.

Lonnie J. White, ed., *Chronicle of a Congressional Journey.* Boulder, CO: Pruett Publishing, 1975. In 1865, Wisconsin Senator James R. Doolittle traveled to Colorado, New Mexico, and elsewhere by order of the U.S. Congress in order to determine the "present condition of the Indian tribes." Samuel B. Davis, a member of the committee accompanying Doolittle, wrote dozens of letters about the journey that are reprinted in this book.

Periodicals

Lyric Wallwork Winik, "We Are Our Destiny," *Parade,* July 18, 1999. An article about the lives and times of Native Americans in the twentieth century printed in *Parade,* a magazine that is a supplement to many Sunday newspapers across the country.

Websites

Hohokam Indians of the Tucson Basin (www.uapress.arizona. edu/online.bks/hohokam/titlhoho.htm). A complete on-line version of the original printed book by Linda M. Gregonis and Karl J. Reinhard that details ancient Hohokam history, lifestyles, and influences on the Southwest.

The Hopi Information Network (www.infomagic.com/~abyte/ hopi/index.htm). Contains links to webpages such as Hopi News Articles; Stories, Teachings, and Prophecies; Visits with the Elders; Help with Hopi Homework Center; Art and Images; Books, Videos, and Publications; Tribal Government Offices; Commerce Center, and more.

The Navajo Central Website (http://navajocentral.org). This collection of over two hundred frequently asked questions about the Navajo tribes provides links to many other Navajo-related sites, including Navajo History, Navajo Rug Weaving, Navajo Code Talkers, Current Events, Tourism Information, and Scenic Wonders.

Pueblo Cultural Center (www.indianpueblo.org). This website contains detailed information about the Pueblo peoples, including history, clan divisions, and more. Links connect to pages about the Acoma, Cochiti, Jemez, Laguna, Taos, Zuni, and other Pueblos.

San Carlos Apache Tribe Cultural Center (www.carizona.com/ super/attractions/san_carlos.html). This site, maintained by members of the San Carlos Apache Reservation, gives a short tribal history and outlines the arts, crafts, artifacts, and other items on display at the cultural center.

Index

Picture Credits

Cover Photo: Tony Stone Images/Paul Chesley
Archive photo, 23, 31, 83
Archive/Hirz photos, 21
Corbis, 35, 38, 78, 82
Corbis/Bettmann, 69
Corbis/Bob Krist, 90
Corbis/David Muench, 15
Corbis/Lee Snider, 86
Corbis/Richard T. Nowitz, 52
Corbis/The Academy of Natural Sciences Philadelphia, 19
Denver Public Library, 85
FPG International, 43, 47, 53, 56, 64, 77
FPG/ Arthur Tilley, 48
FPG/ Bruce Stoddard, 40
FPG/Buddy Mays, 60
FPG/EJ West, 42
FPG/Haroldo Castro, 58
FPG/Harvey Lloyd, 27
FPG/Lee Kuhn, 62
FPG/Michael Goldman, 50
FPG/Richard Price, 29
Library of Congress, 30, 32, 36, 92, 93
North Wind, 7, 9, 10, 41, 44, 45, 70, 71, 75, 81
North Wind/N. Carter, 8, 11, 13, 18, 55, 59
Prints Old and Rare, 66

About the Author

Stuart A. Kallen is the author of more than 145 nonfiction books for children and young adults. He has written on topics ranging from the theory of relativity to rock-and-roll history to life on the American frontier. In addition, Mr. Kallen has written award-winning children's videos and television scripts. In his spare time, Stuart A. Kallen is a singer/songwriter/guitarist in San Diego, California.